SOUND INNOVATIONS

for STRING ORCHESTRA

A Revolutionary Method for Beginning Musicians

Bob **PHILLIPS** | Peter **BOONSHAFT** | Robert **SHELDON**

Congratulations on your decision to play a string instrument!

Making music with family and friends provides enjoyment throughout your lifetime. String instruments are used in all styles of music including classical, fiddling, rock and jazz. You can play in both orchestras and chamber ensembles, as well as community music groups.

Your teacher will help you learn to listen, read, compose, play, analyze and evaluate music. Practicing everyday will help you become an excellent musician. Use the audio recordings and the DVD to help you practice and develop new skills. Playing a string instrument is fun and can lead to a career in music as a performer, composer, teacher, conductor, recording technician and many other music-related jobs.

We wish you the best as you become part of the wonderful world of mu

smartmusic®

mp3 CD

Practice *Sound Innovations* with SmartMusic® Interactive Software

Transform the way you practice. Instead of practicing alone, you play with background accompaniment and hear how your part fits within the whole. *And*, you get instant feedback. You see which notes you've played right or wrong and hear a recording of your performance.

Try SmartMusic today! Get the first 100 lines of music—free—by downloading SmartMusic at **www.smartmusic.com** to get started. Use code SISTRINGS when prompted during the activation process.

The MP3 CD includes recorded accompaniments for every line of music in your *Sound Innovations* book. These instrument-specific recordings can be played with the included SI Player, easily uploaded to your MP3 player or transferred to your computer. Additionally, many CD and DVD players are equipped to play MP3s directly from the disc. To play an accompaniment, simply choose the file that corresponds to the line of music in the book. Each line has been numbered and named for easy reference.

Also included on the MP3 CD is the SI Player *with* Tempo Change Technology. The SI Player features the ability to change the speed of the recordings without changing pitch—slow the tempo down for practice or speed it up to performance tempo! Use this program to easily play the included MP3 files or any audio file on your computer.

SI Player can be launched directly from the MP3 CD or from your computer's hard drive. To launch the SI Player from the CD, simply double-click the SI Player application on the disc. For better performance (on machines with slower CD drives) run the SI Player from your computer's hard drive. To do this, select both folders on the CD and copy them to a directory on your computer. Note: It is important that these folders be located within the same directory for the program to function properly once installed. Do not rename the folder of MP3 files.

Alfred

ISBN-10: 0-7390-6787-7
ISBN-13: 978-0-7390-6787-1

Instrument photos courtesy of Yamaha Corporation of America Band & Orchestral Division

Instrumentation

Teacher's Score

Violin

Viola

Cello

Bass

Piano Accompaniment

About the Authors

Bob Phillips

Pedagogue, composer, and teacher trainer, Bob Phillips is renowned as a leader in music education and is the lead author of *SI for String Orchestra*. During his 27 years teaching strings and winds in Michigan, Phillips built a thriving orchestra program that was a national model of excellence. A recognized expert in the use of large group pedagogy, he has presented clinics throughout the nation and around the world. Phillips has authored more than 50 books including Alfred's Philharmonic series. His conducting resumé includes professional, all-state, and youth orchestras and he currently serves as Director of String Publications for Alfred and President-Elect of the American String Teachers Association.

Peter Boonshaft

Hailed as one of the most exciting and exhilarating voices in music education today, Peter Boonshaft has been a guest clinician in every state in the U.S., as well as internationally. He is the author of the critically acclaimed books *Teaching Music with Passion*, *Teaching Music with Purpose*, and *Teaching Music with Promise*. Having taught for 29 years, he is currently on the faculty of Hofstra University In Hempstead, New York. Dr. Boonshaft has received honors from political leaders around the world and has been selected three times as a National Endowment for the Arts "Artist in Residence."

Robert Sheldon

Well-known composer/music educator and lead author of *SI for Concert Band*, Robert Sheldon has taught instrumental music in the Florida and Illinois public schools, and has served on the faculty at Florida State Univeristy. As Concert Band Editor for Alfred, he maintains an active composition and conducting schedule, and regularly accepts commissions for new works. An internationally recognized clinician, Sheldon has conducted numerous Regional and All-State Honors Bands throughout the United States and abroad.

String Skills

SOUND INNOVATIONS for STRING ORCHESTRA	Page 3 & Sound Notation	Sound Beginnings (Level 1)	Sound Fundamentals (Level 2)	Sound Musicianship (Level 3)	Sound Techniques (Level 4)	Sound Development (Level 5)	Sound Performance (Level 6)
Rhythms	♩ 𝅝 𝄽 / 4/4	♩ (half note) 𝄺 / ♫ (eighth notes) ♬ (sixteenth notes)	2/4 / 3/4 / 𝅗𝅥. / C / Tie / Pickup	𝅝 𝄻		♪ / 𝄾 / 𝅘𝅥𝅮.	
Left-Hand Technique	(staff) / ♯ / ♭ / ♮ / 𝄞 / Ledger Line	Key of D Major / D Major Scale	Arpeggio / Chord / Half Step / Whole Step / Key of G Major / G Major Scale / Left-Hand Pizzicato	Key of C Major / C Major Scale / Chromatics / Courtesy Accidental	Major Keys / Minor Keys		Pentatonic Scale
Right-Hand Technique	Pizzicato (page 3)	Arco / ' / ⊓ / ∨ / Bow Hold / Placing the Bow / Bowing Lanes / Moving the Bow / Levels of the Bow / String Crossings / Bow Speed	Slur / Hooked Bowing / Using Different Parts of the Bow			Double Stops	
Sequence & Tempo	(staff braces)	1st & 2nd Endings	D.C. al Fine / Fine / Andante / Moderato / Allegro	Rehearsal Marks		⌢ (fermata) / Rallentando / Ritardando	
Style		Theme	Round / Harmony / Duet / Staccato / Tenuto / Legato	*f* / *mf* / *p* / Improvisation	*f–p*	< / >	Orchestra Arrangment / Solo

Chart of Sequential Introduction of Notes

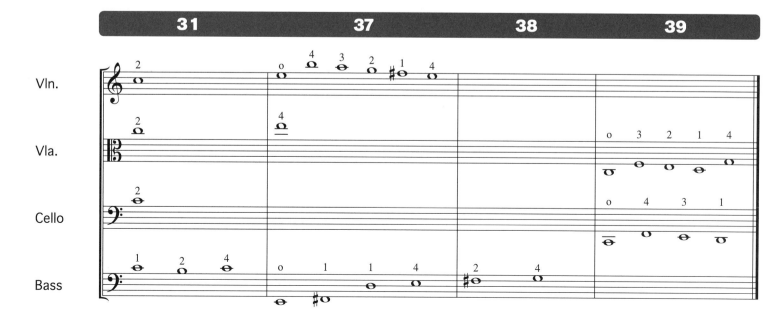

Features

We all know how important the choice of a method book is to you and your students, and we are delighted you have chosen Alfred Music Publishing's *Sound Innovations for String Orchestra*. Years of research, listening to the concerns of teachers about what they wanted and didn't want in a method book, led to this extraordinary new approach. Here are some of the features you will find:

▶ **Uncluttered page layouts**

▶ **Clear introductions of new concepts**

▶ **Use of rhythmic counting system, including subdivisions**

▶ **Unique grey-scale counting system for rests to encourage counting**

▶ **Preparation of all new rhythms**

▶ **Clearly-stated goals for exercises throughout the book so students understand their purpose**

▶ **Six levels serving as benchmarks for progress and motivation**

▶ ***Sound Checks* at the end of each level for assessment**

▶ **Fingering graphics next to each new note**

▶ **Opportunities to teach performance through solos, duets, rounds, and large ensemble pieces in diverse musical styles**

▶ **Opportunities to teach improvisation, history, composition and conducting**

▶ **Masterclass DVDs included with each book**

- Instrument specific
- Taught by expert studio teachers who are inviting and engaging
- Filmed in HD
- Covers basic and more advanced skills throughout the entire book
- Includes a complete performance of the final solo
- Encourages students to watch at home to reinforce learning

▶ **MP3 audio recordings included with each book**

- Instrument specific
- Every line in the book is recorded on one CD
- All recorded track numbers match the line numbers of each book
- Recordings of melody with accompaniment, then accompaniment alone
- Includes full string orchestra recordings for all large ensemble pieces
- Accompaniments are in varied styles, including classical
- Synthesized accompaniments make it easy for students to hear the melody
- Includes instrument-specific tuning note of each string on the first and last track of each CD
- Tempo changer is included on the same disk

▶ **A glossary in each student book**

▶ **Fingering chart for each instrument**

▶ **Correlated performance series, including Educational Pack, written by the composer**

▶ **Entire book is available on *SmartMusic***

- Access to the first 100 Lines of the book is free without subscription

▶ **Online community for teachers to share ideas**

▶ **Teacher's book includes:**

- All masterclass DVDs
- All accompaniment MP3 CDs
- *Sound Advice* teaching tips
- A separate CD with the final solo of each instrument for teaching characteristic tone
- A list of National Standards
- A reproducible practice record and Certificate of Completion

Sound Innovations for String Orchestra
DIRECTOR'S CHOICE EDITION

This revolution in beginning string methods allows you to customize your own book that matches your philosophy and pedagogical approach.

Simply go to **www.alfred.com/soundinnovations**:

▶ **Create your own book profile**

▶ **Select arco or pizzicato**

▶ **Select notes ascending or descending**

▶ **Select your starting rhythm**

▶ **Choose to include note names inside the note heads (and for how many pages) or not**

▶ **Personalize the cover with your name and your school's name**

▶ **Add your own welcome letter**

▶ **Select individual tunes or choose tunes by genre (including world music, classical, Latino, pop, Christian, African-American, Texas, Canadian, and many more)**

▶ **Add enrichment pages for additional practice to reinforce what has been learned with no new material (such as technique and rhythm, additional tunes, history, theory, composition, improvisation, duets and ensembles, assessment pages, finger twisters, and scales)**

▶ **Every teacher in a school district can create their own book knowing students will end in the same place no matter how each book was customized**

▶ **If you teach homogeneously, you can even customize a book for each instrument class**

▶ **The printed book is shipped directly to you with all customization and enrichment pages matching exactly to the accompaniment CD, Teacher's Book, and *SmartMusic***

Sound Innovations offers opportunities to expand and enhance student learning and understanding through creative teaching. Having students sing exercises throughout the book communicates the value of this essential skill, as well as fosters the development of intonation and musicianship in their instrumental performance. Selecting tunes for students to play by ear can help them develop this vital aspect of musical facility. Once students are comfortable with the composition and improvisation exercises in the book, suggest they repeat them using different keys, and that they compose or improvise a variety of rhythmic passages, accompaniments and melodies.

An understanding of music is vital to the education of every child. Through music, students develop their abilities of expression, imagination, analysis, creativity, self-discipline, teamwork, evaluative methods, and critical thinking. Music also reinforces, augments and gives students a lens with which to view and interpret other subjects contributing to a well-rounded education. As educators, we help young people discover how music relates to other academic subjects, such as mathematics, writing, foreign language, reading, physical education, drama, dance, history, social studies, creative writing, and the sciences. Remember to communicate to students, parents, and administrators the broad scope and impact of music on the development and education of the whole child.

VIOLIN

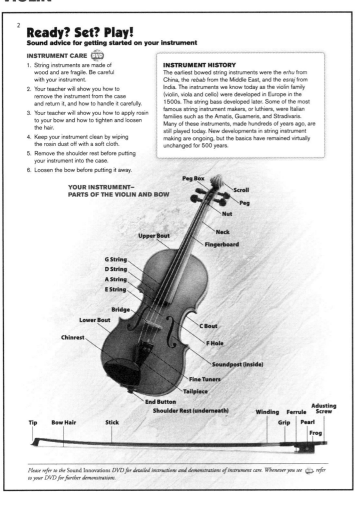

² ## Ready? Set? Play!
Sound advice for getting started on your instrument

INSTRUMENT CARE (DVD)

1. String instruments are made of wood and are fragile. Be careful with your instrument.
2. Your teacher will show you how to remove the instrument from the case and return it, and how to handle it carefully.
3. Your teacher will show you how to apply rosin to your bow and how to tighten and loosen the hair.
4. Keep your instrument clean by wiping the rosin dust off with a soft cloth.
5. Remove the shoulder rest before putting your instrument into the case.
6. Loosen the bow before putting it away.

INSTRUMENT HISTORY

The earliest bowed string instruments were the *erhu* from China, the *rebab* from the Middle East, and the *esraj* from India. The instruments we know today as the violin family (violin, viola and cello) were developed in Europe in the 1500s. The string bass developed later. Some of the most famous string instrument makers, or luthiers, were Italian families such as the Amatis, Guarneris, and Stradivaris. Many of these instruments, made hundreds of years ago, are still played today. New developments in string instrument making are ongoing, but the basics have remained virtually unchanged for 500 years.

YOUR INSTRUMENT—PARTS OF THE VIOLIN AND BOW

Peg Box, Scroll, Peg, Nut, Neck, Fingerboard, Upper Bout, G String, D String, A String, E String, Bridge, Lower Bout, C Bout, Chinrest, F Hole, Soundpost (inside), Fine Tuners, Tailpiece, End Button, Shoulder Rest (underneath), Winding, Ferrule, Adjusting Screw, Grip, Pearl, Frog, Tip, Bow Hair, Stick

Please refer to the Sound Innovations DVD for detailed instructions and demonstrations of instrument care. Whenever you see (DVD), refer to your DVD for further demonstrations.

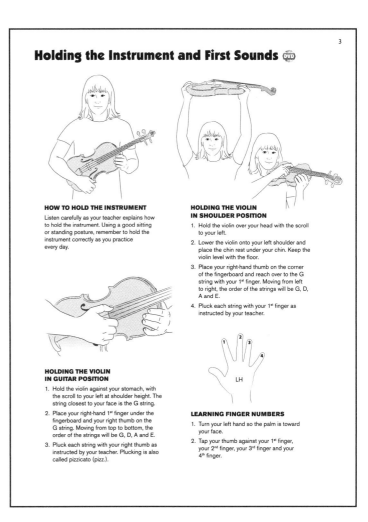

³ ## Holding the Instrument and First Sounds (DVD)

HOW TO HOLD THE INSTRUMENT

Listen carefully as your teacher explains how to hold the instrument. Using a good sitting or standing posture, remember to hold the instrument correctly as you practice every day.

HOLDING THE VIOLIN IN SHOULDER POSITION

1. Hold the violin over your head with the scroll to your left.
2. Lower the violin onto your left shoulder and place the chin rest under your chin. Keep the violin level with the floor.
3. Place your right-hand thumb on the corner of the fingerboard and reach over to the G string with your 1st finger. Moving from left to right, the order of the strings will be G, D, A and E.
4. Pluck each string with your 1st finger as instructed by your teacher.

HOLDING THE VIOLIN IN GUITAR POSITION

1. Hold the violin against your stomach, with the scroll to your left at shoulder height. The string closest to your face is the G string.
2. Place your right-hand 1st finger under the fingerboard and your right thumb on the G string. Moving from top to bottom, the order of the strings will be G, D, A and E.
3. Pluck each string with your right thumb as instructed by your teacher. Plucking is also called pizzicato (pizz.).

LH

LEARNING FINGER NUMBERS

1. Turn your left hand so the palm is toward your face.
2. Tap your thumb against your 1st finger, your 2nd finger, your 3rd finger and your 4th finger.

VIOLA

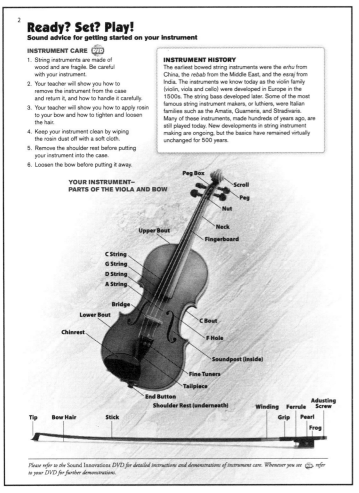

² ## Ready? Set? Play!
Sound advice for getting started on your instrument

INSTRUMENT CARE (DVD)

1. String instruments are made of wood and are fragile. Be careful with your instrument.
2. Your teacher will show you how to remove the instrument from the case and return it, and how to handle it carefully.
3. Your teacher will show you how to apply rosin to your bow and how to tighten and loosen the hair.
4. Keep your instrument clean by wiping the rosin dust off with a soft cloth.
5. Remove the shoulder rest before putting your instrument into the case.
6. Loosen the bow before putting it away.

INSTRUMENT HISTORY

The earliest bowed string instruments were the *erhu* from China, the *rebab* from the Middle East, and the *esraj* from India. The instruments we know today as the violin family (violin, viola and cello) were developed in Europe in the 1500s. The string bass developed later. Some of the most famous string instrument makers, or luthiers, were Italian families such as the Amatis, Guarneris, and Stradivaris. Many of these instruments, made hundreds of years ago, are still played today. New developments in string instrument making are ongoing, but the basics have remained virtually unchanged for 500 years.

YOUR INSTRUMENT—PARTS OF THE VIOLA AND BOW

Peg Box, Scroll, Peg, Nut, Neck, Fingerboard, Upper Bout, C String, G String, D String, A String, Bridge, Lower Bout, C Bout, Chinrest, F Hole, Soundpost (inside), Fine Tuners, Tailpiece, End Button, Shoulder Rest (underneath), Winding, Ferrule, Adjusting Screw, Grip, Pearl, Frog, Tip, Bow Hair, Stick

Please refer to the Sound Innovations DVD for detailed instructions and demonstrations of instrument care. Whenever you see (DVD), refer to your DVD for further demonstrations.

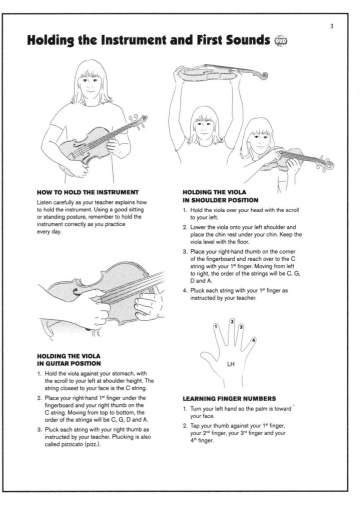

³ ## Holding the Instrument and First Sounds (DVD)

HOW TO HOLD THE INSTRUMENT

Listen carefully as your teacher explains how to hold the instrument. Using a good sitting or standing posture, remember to hold the instrument correctly as you practice every day.

HOLDING THE VIOLA IN SHOULDER POSITION

1. Hold the viola over your head with the scroll to your left.
2. Lower the viola onto your left shoulder and place the chin rest under your chin. Keep the viola level with the floor.
3. Place your right-hand thumb on the corner of the fingerboard and reach over to the C string with your 1st finger. Moving from left to right, the order of the strings will be C, G, D and A.
4. Pluck each string with your 1st finger as instructed by your teacher.

HOLDING THE VIOLA IN GUITAR POSITION

1. Hold the viola against your stomach, with the scroll to your left at shoulder height. The string closest to your face is the C string.
2. Place your right-hand 1st finger under the fingerboard and your right thumb on the C string. Moving from top to bottom, the order of the strings will be C, G, D and A.
3. Pluck each string with your right thumb as instructed by your teacher. Plucking is also called pizzicato (pizz.).

LH

LEARNING FINGER NUMBERS

1. Turn your left hand so the palm is toward your face.
2. Tap your thumb against your 1st finger, your 2nd finger, your 3rd finger and your 4th finger.

CELLO

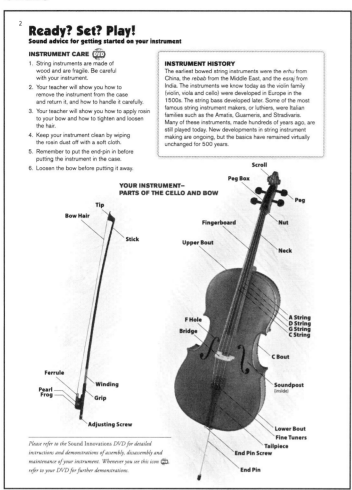

2

Ready? Set? Play!
Sound advice for getting started on your instrument

INSTRUMENT CARE 🔘DVD

1. String instruments are made of wood and are fragile. Be careful with your instrument.

2. Your teacher will show you how to remove the instrument from the case and return it, and how to handle it carefully.

3. Your teacher will show you how to apply rosin to your bow and how to tighten and loosen the hair.

4. Keep your instrument clean by wiping the rosin dust off with a soft cloth.

5. Remember to put the end-pin in before putting the instrument in the case.

6. Loosen the bow before putting it away.

INSTRUMENT HISTORY

The earliest bowed string instruments were the *erhu* from China, the *rebab* from the Middle East, and the *esraj* from India. The instruments we know today as the violin family (violin, viola and cello) were developed in Europe in the 1500s. The string bass developed later. Some of the most famous string instrument makers, or luthiers, were Italian families such as the Amatis, Guarneris, and Stradivaris. Many of these instruments, made hundreds of years ago, are still played today. New developments in string instrument making are ongoing, but the basics have remained virtually unchanged for 500 years.

YOUR INSTRUMENT–PARTS OF THE CELLO AND BOW

Tip
Bow Hair
Stick
Scroll
Peg Box
Peg
Fingerboard
Nut
Upper Bout
Neck
Ferrule
Pearl Frog
Winding
Grip
Adjusting Screw
F Hole
Bridge
A String
D String
G String
C String
C Bout
Soundpost (inside)
Lower Bout
Fine Tuners
Tailpiece
End Pin Screw
End Pin

Please refer to the Sound Innovations DVD for detailed instructions and demonstrations of assembly, disassembly and maintenance of your instrument. Whenever you see this icon 🔘, refer to your DVD for further demonstrations.

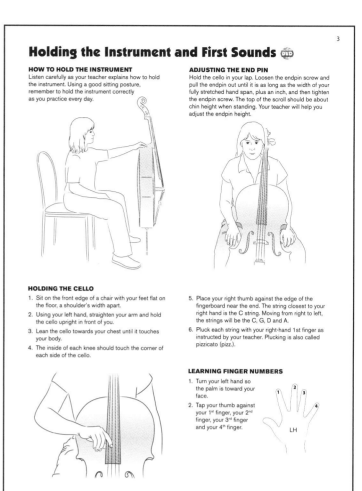

3

Holding the Instrument and First Sounds 🔘DVD

HOW TO HOLD THE INSTRUMENT
Listen carefully as your teacher explains how to hold the instrument. Using a good sitting posture, remember to hold the instrument correctly as you practice every day.

ADJUSTING THE END PIN
Hold the cello in your lap. Loosen the endpin screw and pull the endpin out until it is as long as the width of your fully stretched hand span, plus an inch, and then tighten the endpin screw. The top of the scroll should be about chin height when standing. Your teacher will help you adjust the endpin height.

HOLDING THE CELLO

1. Sit on the front edge of a chair with your feet flat on the floor, a shoulder's width apart.

2. Using your left hand, straighten your arm and hold the cello upright in front of you.

3. Lean the cello towards your chest until it touches your body.

4. The inside of each knee should touch the corner of each side of the cello.

5. Place your right thumb against the edge of the fingerboard near the end. The string closest to your right hand is the C string. Moving from right to left, the strings will be the C, G, D and A.

6. Pluck each string with your right-hand 1st finger as instructed by your teacher. Plucking is also called pizzicato (pizz.).

LEARNING FINGER NUMBERS

1. Turn your left hand so the palm is toward your face.

2. Tap your thumb against your 1st finger, your 2nd finger, your 3rd finger and your 4th finger.

LH

BASS

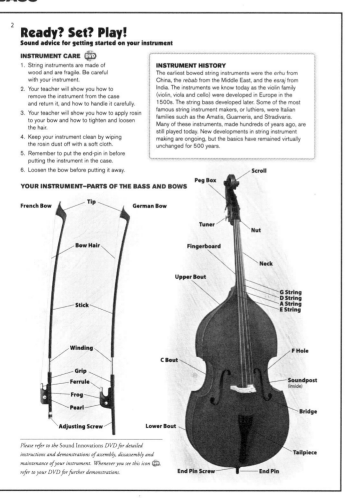

2

Ready? Set? Play!
Sound advice for getting started on your instrument

INSTRUMENT CARE 🔘DVD

1. String instruments are made of wood and are fragile. Be careful with your instrument.

2. Your teacher will show you how to remove the instrument from the case and return it, and how to handle it carefully.

3. Your teacher will show you how to apply rosin to your bow and how to tighten and loosen the hair.

4. Keep your instrument clean by wiping the rosin dust off with a soft cloth.

5. Remember to put the end-pin in before putting the instrument in the case.

6. Loosen the bow before putting it away.

INSTRUMENT HISTORY

The earliest bowed string instruments were the *erhu* from China, the *rebab* from the Middle East, and the *esraj* from India. The instruments we know today as the violin family (violin, viola and cello) were developed in Europe in the 1500s. The string bass developed later. Some of the most famous string instrument makers, or luthiers, were Italian families such as the Amatis, Guarneris, and Stradivaris. Many of these instruments, made hundreds of years ago, are still played today. New developments in string instrument making are ongoing, but the basics have remained virtually unchanged for 500 years.

YOUR INSTRUMENT–PARTS OF THE BASS AND BOWS

French Bow
Tip
German Bow
Bow Hair
Stick
Winding
Grip
Ferrule
Frog
Pearl
Adjusting Screw
Scroll
Peg Box
Tuner
Nut
Fingerboard
Neck
Upper Bout
G String
D String
A String
E String
C Bout
F Hole
Soundpost (inside)
Bridge
Lower Bout
Tailpiece
End Pin Screw
End Pin

Please refer to the Sound Innovations DVD for detailed instructions and demonstration of assembly, disassembly and maintenance of your instrument. Whenever you see this icon 🔘, refer to your DVD for further demonstrations.

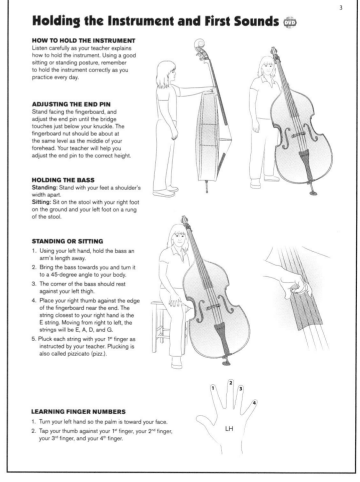

3

Holding the Instrument and First Sounds 🔘DVD

HOW TO HOLD THE INSTRUMENT
Listen carefully as your teacher explains how to hold the instrument. Using a good sitting or standing posture, remember to hold the instrument correctly as you practice every day.

ADJUSTING THE END PIN
Stand facing the fingerboard, and adjust the end pin until the bridge touches just below your knuckle. The fingerboard nut should be about at the same level as the middle of your forehead. Your teacher will help you adjust the end pin to the correct height.

HOLDING THE BASS
Standing: Stand with your feet a shoulder's width apart.
Sitting: Sit on the stool with your right foot on the ground and your left foot on a rung of the stool.

STANDING OR SITTING

1. Using your left hand, hold the bass an arm's length away.

2. Bring the bass towards you and turn it to a 45-degree angle to your body.

3. The corner of the bass should rest against your left thigh.

4. Place your right thumb against the edge of the fingerboard near the end. The string closest to your right hand is the E string. Moving from right to left, the strings will be E, A, D, and G.

5. Pluck each string with your 1st finger as instructed by your teacher. Plucking is also called pizzicato (pizz.).

LEARNING FINGER NUMBERS

1. Turn your left hand so the palm is toward your face.

2. Tap your thumb against your 1st finger, your 2nd finger, your 3rd finger, and your 4th finger.

LH

VIOLIN

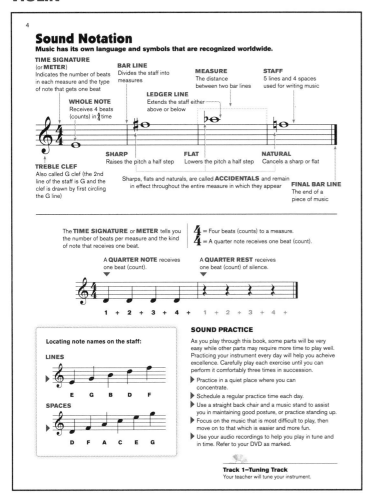

VIOLA

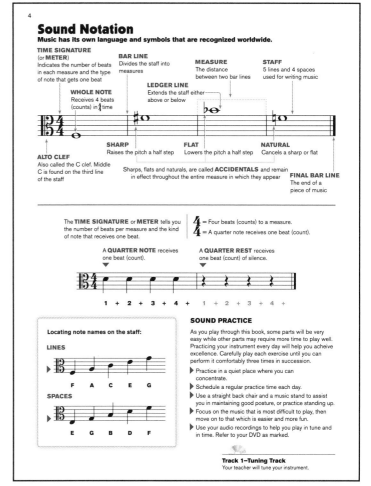

CELLO/BASS

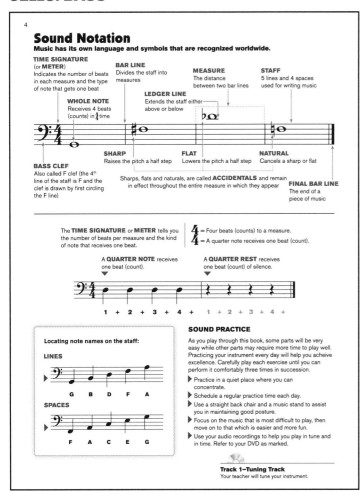

National Standards for Music Education

1. Singing, alone and with others, a varied repertoire of music.

2. Performing on instruments, alone and with others, a varied repertoire of music.

3. Improvising melodies, variations, and accompaniments.

4. Composing and arranging music within specified guidelines.

5. Reading and notating music.

6. Listening to, analyzing, and describing music.

7. Evaluating music and music performances.

8. Understanding relationships between music, the other arts, and disciplines outside the arts.

9. Understanding music in relation to history and culture.

Level 1: Sound Beginnings

Introduction and Tuning
Your teacher will tune your instrument.

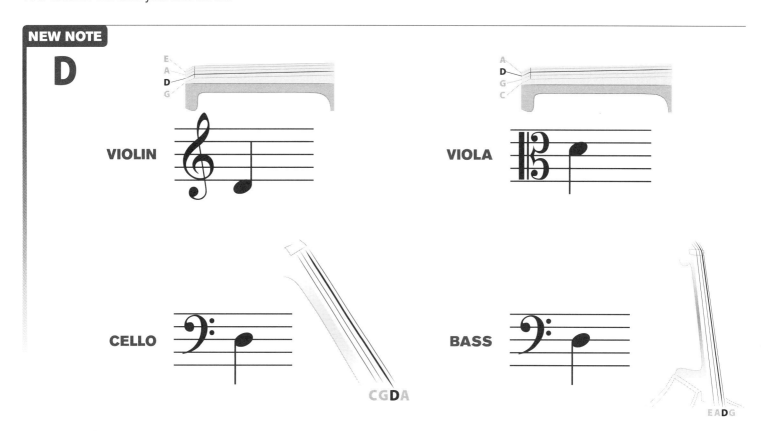

NEW NOTE

D

VIOLIN   VIOLA

CELLO   BASS

2   **NEW NOTE OPEN D STRING**—*Listen as your teacher counts, claps, then plays the D string, echoing back each time.*

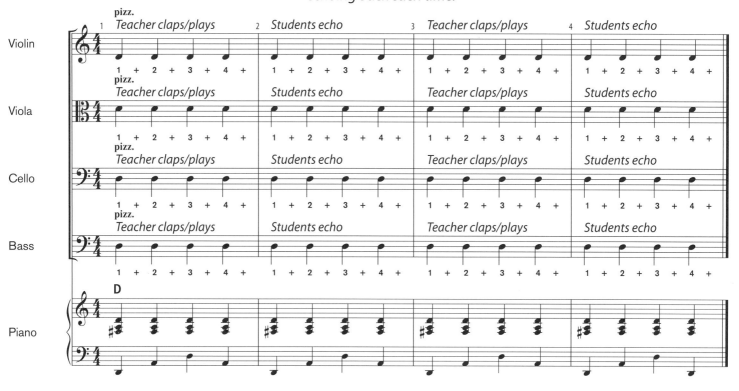

SOUND ADVICE

Remind students to use the Accompaniment CD when practicing and to use the DVD whenever the icon appears.

3   ## OPEN D STRING PIZZ-N-PLUCK—*Learn to pluck the open (o) D string as you count, clap, sing and then pluck the piece.*

SOUND ADVICE

Explain to students that the o above the note indicates a fingering.

NEW NOTE

A

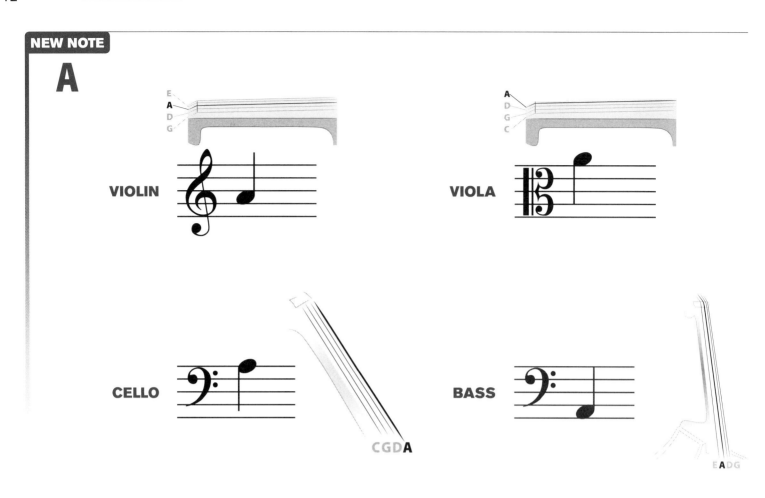

4 **NEW NOTE OPEN A STRING**—*Learn to pluck the open (o) A string as you count, clap, sing and then pluck the piece.*

SOUND ADVICE

Remind students to maintain a good posture while playing.

5 **RESTING PIZZ.**—*Learn to pluck the open (o) D and open (o) A strings as you clap, sing and then pluck the piece.*

SOUND ADVICE

Remind students to prepare to move to the A string during the rests in bar 2.

6 **CROSSING D TO A**—*Learn to go from the D to the A string as you clap, sing and then pluck the piece.*

SOUND ADVICE

Remind students that the piece is not complete until they count the rest on the last beat of bar 4.

7   **CROSSING A TO D**—*Learn to go from the A to the D string as you clap, sing and then pluck the piece.*

SOUND ADVICE

Remind students to play with a steady tempo throughout the entire line.

PLACING FINGERS ON THE D STRING

LEFT-HAND SETUP DVD

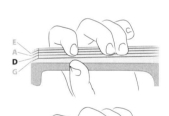

VIOLIN/ VIOLA
1. Place your left hand at the neck near the nut, keeping your wrist relaxed and straight.
2. Put three fingers on the D string (fingertips touching the string).
3. Your fingers should be curved.
4. The base of your 1st finger will touch the neck.
5. Your 1st finger will make a square over the fingerboard.
6. When your fingers are not on the string, keep them close to the string.
7. Tap your thumb against the neck and make sure it is relaxed.

CELLO
1. Place your left hand at the neck approximately three to four inches from the nut, keeping your wrist relaxed and straight.
2. Put four fingers on the D string (pads of the finger touching the string).
3. Your fingers should be curved.
4. Your thumb should be opposite your 2nd finger.
5. Your left arm should be at a 45-degree angle to the floor.
6. When your fingers are not on the string, keep them close to the string.
7. Tap your thumb against the neck and make sure it is relaxed.

BASS
1. Place your left hand at the neck approximately four to five inches from the nut, keeping your wrist relaxed and straight.
2. Put four fingers on the D string (pads of the finger touching the string).
3. Your fingers should be curved.
4. Your thumb should be opposite your 2nd finger.
5. Your elbow should be up and off the bass.
6. When your fingers are not on the string, keep them close to the string.
7. Tap your thumb against the neck and make sure it is relaxed.

SOUND ADVICE

Remind students to watch the DVD whenever they see the DVD icon to reinforce the learning of new concepts.

NEW NOTE

G

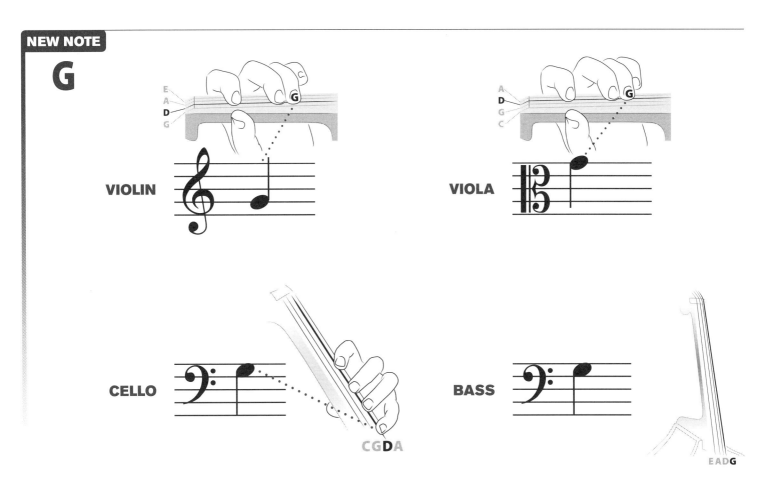

VIOLIN

VIOLA

CELLO

BASS

8   **NEW NOTE G**—*Learn to play G on the D string for violins, violas and cellos. Basses learn the open G string.*

SOUND ADVICE

Remind students to keep the left-hand wrist straight, and to watch the DVD to review tips on finger placement.

9   **G AND D JUMPS**—*Learn how to move between G and D, and then back again.*

SOUND ADVICE

Remind students to keep the left-hand fingers close to the fingerboard while playing the open strings.

NEW NOTE

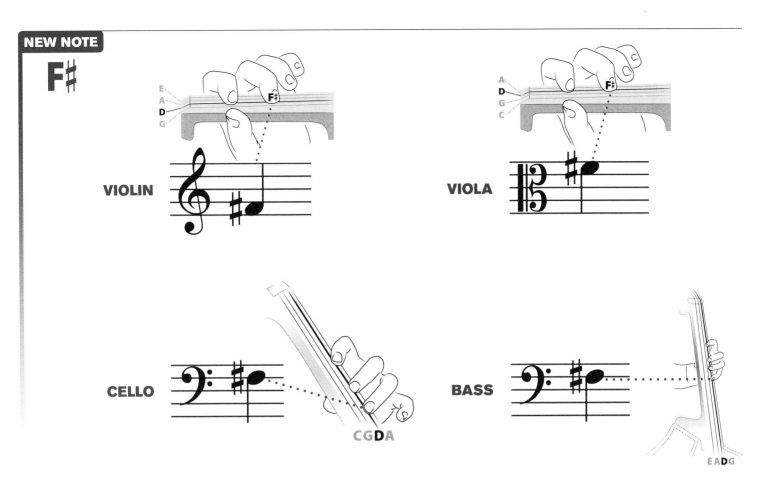

10   **NEW NOTE F#**—*Learn to play F# on the D string.*

SOUND ADVICE

Remind students to place the left-hand fingers firmly on the string. They should feel the weight of their hand sink into the string.

18

11 **F♯ AND D JUMPS**—*Learn to move between F♯ and D, and then back again.*

SOUND ADVICE

Remind students to clap each new exercise before they play it.

NEW NOTE

E

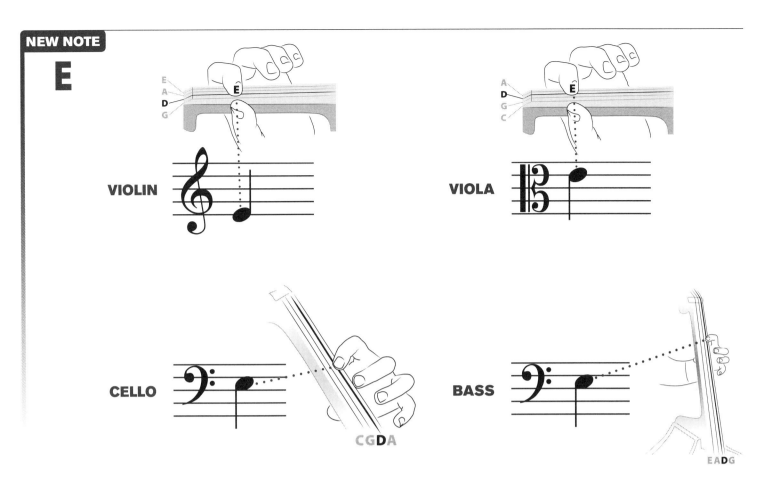

VIOLIN

VIOLA

CELLO

CGD**A**

BASS

E**ADG**

12   **NEW NOTE E**—*Learn to play E on the D string.*

SOUND ADVICE

Have half the ensemble clap the rhythm of this tune while the other half plays, then reverse.

13   **E AND D JUMPS**—*Learn to move between E and D, and then back again.*

SOUND ADVICE

Remind students that feet remain flat on the floor.

14   **DOWN, DOWN**—*Play notes that go down in pitch on the D string. Basses start with the G string.*

SOUND ADVICE

Remind students to prepare to lift the left-hand fingers during the rests.

15   **CLIMBING, CLIMBING**—*Play notes that go up in pitch on the D string. Basses end with the open G string.*

SOUND ADVICE

Remind students to prepare to place the left-hand fingers before each new measure.

16   **DOWN AND UP**—*Practice walking your fingers down and then up the D string.*

SOUND ADVICE

Remind students to relax the left hand while playing this exercise.

17 **JOLLY FELLOWS**—*This melody (tune) continues on the next staff. Notice that the second line does not need to show the meter.*

Slavonic Folk Song

SOUND ADVICE

Point out that the piece continues onto a second line of music.

Many American fiddle tunes, such as *Boil Them Cabbage Down*, came from the Scottish-Irish tradition and changed over time into an American style of fiddling.

18

BOIL THEM CABBAGE DOWN—*Before playing, write the name of the first note in each measure.*

American Folk Song

SOUND ADVICE

It is never too early for students to have their first concert. Perform *Boil Them Cabbage Down* as if it were a concert. Let students perform for each other.

PLACING FINGERS ON THE A STRING (G STRING FOR BASSES) DVD

NEW NOTE

D

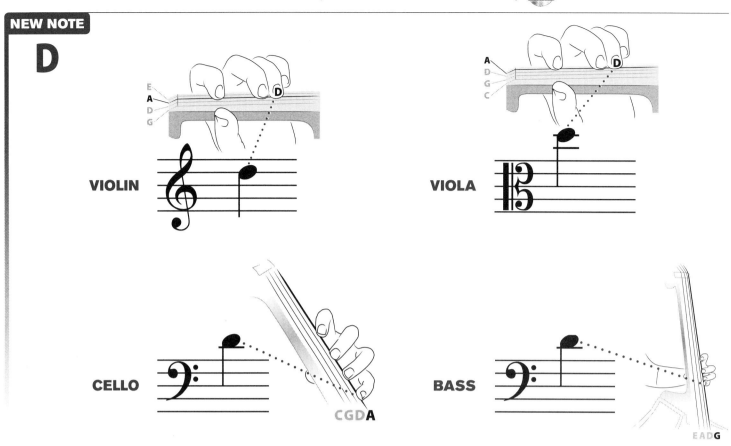

VIOLIN

VIOLA

CELLO

BASS

19 **NEW NOTE D**—*Learn to play D on the A string for violins, violas and cellos. Basses learn D . Reminder:* **LEDGER LINES** *are short, horizontal lines used to extend a staff either higher or lower.*

SOUND ADVICE

Explain that this D is an octave above the open D. Have students listen to the open string and then the octave D. Remind them to watch the DVD for tips on finger placement.

D AND A JUMPS—*Learn to move between D and A.*

SOUND ADVICE

Have half the students clap the rhythm while the other half plays, then switch.

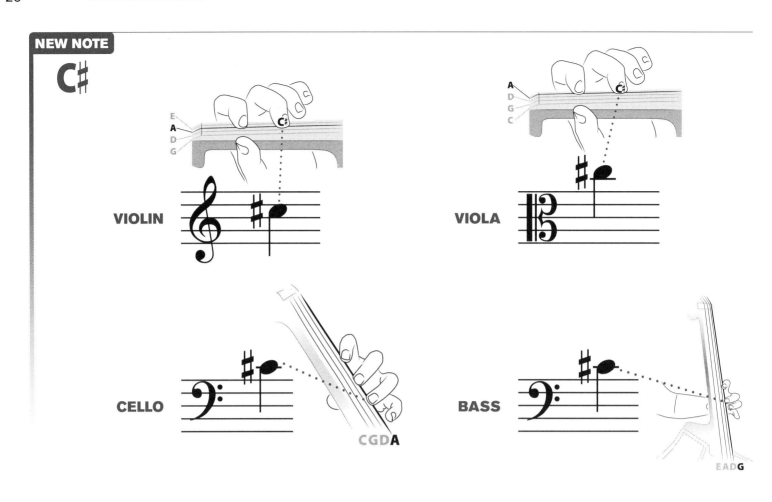

NEW NOTE

C♯

VIOLIN

VIOLA

CELLO

BASS

21 **NEW NOTE C♯**—*Learn to play C♯ on the A string for violins, violas and cellos. Basses play C♯ on the G string.*

SOUND ADVICE

Remind students that the left-hand fingers should be rounded or curved.

C♯ AND A JUMPS—*Learn to move between C♯ and A.*

SOUND ADVICE

Remind students to always play with a good sound.

NEW NOTE

B

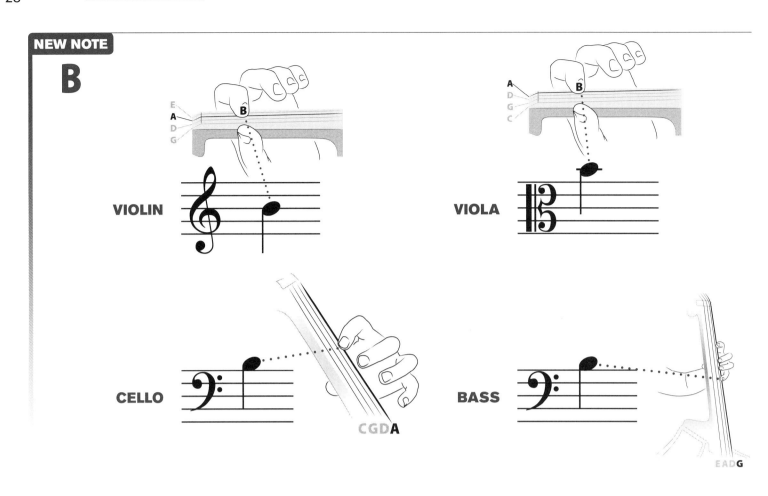

VIOLIN

VIOLA

CELLO

BASS

23

NEW NOTE B—*Learn to play B on the A string for violins, violas and cellos. Basses play B on the G string.*

SOUND ADVICE

Remind students to maintain a straight back when sitting or standing.

NEW NOTE FOR BASSES

A

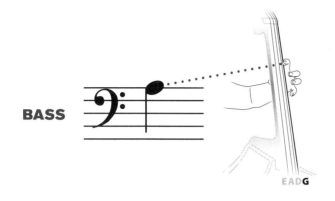

BASS

24 **NEW NOTE A FOR BASSES**—*Learn to move between B and A. Basses learn to play A on the G string.*

SOUND ADVICE

The basses will be learning 1st finger A on the G string while everyone else reviews A and B.

25   **A-DOWN WE GO**—*Practice walking down the A string. G string for basses.*

SOUND ADVICE

Ask students if this exercise sounds similar to *Down, Down*.

26   **AND UP WE GO**—*Practice walking up the A string. G string for basses.*

SOUND ADVICE

Ask students if this exercise sounds similar to *Climbing, Climbing*.

27   **UP AND DOWN THE LADDER**—*Practice walking up and down the A string. G string for basses.*

SOUND ADVICE

Remind students to leave the left-hand fingers down as long as possible while ascending.

28 **AU CLAIRE DE LA LUNE**—*Before playing this piece, write the names of the notes on the lines.*

French Folk Song

SOUND ADVICE

Have students sing the song before playing.

A **SCALE** usually consists of a series of eight notes that go up or down the musical alphabet in a specific order of whole steps and half steps. The lowest and highest notes of the scale are always the same letter name.

29 **GOING DOWN THE D SCALE**—*Use all the notes on the A and D strings. Write the names of the notes on the lines. G and D strings for basses*

SOUND ADVICE

Explain to students what a scale is and why it is important to learn scales.

30   GOING UP THE D SCALE—*Now play each note of the scale twice.*

SOUND ADVICE

Remind students to move the left-hand fingers quickly. This scale changes pitch every two beats, which is twice as fast as *Going Down the D Scale*.

31   PLAYING UP AND DOWN THE D SCALE—*Play the notes going up the scale and then come back down without stopping.*

SOUND ADVICE

Explain to students that when scales are performed, sometimes the top note is repeated and sometimes it is not.

VIOLIN

A **KEY SIGNATURE** appears at the beginning of the staff. It tells you which notes will be played sharp or flat. This key signature tells you that all F's and C's are played as F♯ and C♯. It is called the key of D major.

VIOLA

A **KEY SIGNATURE** appears at the beginning of the staff. It tells you which notes will be played sharp or flat. This key signature tells you that all F's and C's are played as F♯ and C♯. It is called the key of D major.

CELLO/BASS

A **KEY SIGNATURE** appears at the beginning of the staff. It tells you which notes will be played sharp or flat. This key signature tells you that all F's and C's are played as F♯ and C♯. It is called the key of D major.

A **THEME** is a central musical idea or melody.

A **COMPOSER** is a person who writes music.

Wolfgang Amadeus Mozart (1756–1791) wrote 12 variations on the French folk song *Ah vous diraj-je, maman*, in 1781. English words were added in 1806 and the song was retitled *Twinkle, Twinkle Little Star.*

32 **TWINKLE, TWINKLE LITTLE STAR**—*Listen to the recording and identify theme A and theme B.*

SOUND ADVICE

While students listen to the recording, ask them to raise a hand each time a new theme is played.

VIOLIN
SETTING UP THE RIGHT HAND WITH A PENCIL

1. Hold a pencil in your left hand, with the pencil point facing toward the left. Let the fingers of your right hand hang over the pencil.

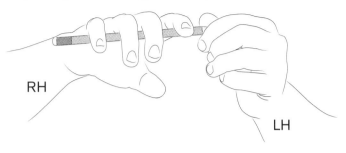

2. Let the tip of your 4th finger rest on top of the pencil by the eraser.

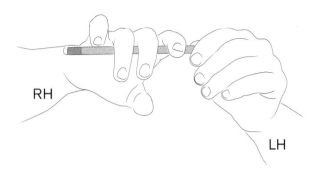

3. Curve or hook your right thumb and place the tip of the thumb on the pencil underneath your right-hand 2nd finger.

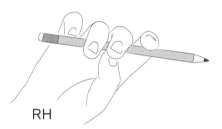

4. Let go with your left hand and rock the pencil back and forth by using your 1st finger and 4th finger.

VIOLA
SETTING UP THE RIGHT HAND WITH A PENCIL

1. Hold a pencil in your left hand, with the pencil point facing toward the left. Let the fingers of your right hand hang over the pencil.

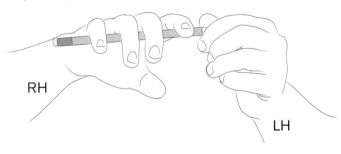

2. Let the tip of your 4th finger rest on top of the pencil by the eraser.

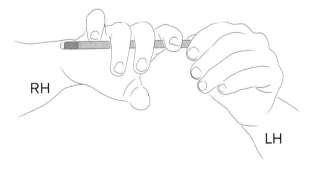

3. Curve or hook your right thumb and place the tip of the thumb on the pencil underneath your right-hand 2nd finger.

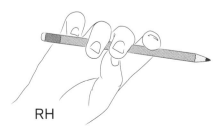

4. Let go with your left hand and rock the pencil back and forth by using your 1st finger and 4th finger.

CELLO
SETTING UP THE RIGHT HAND WITH A PENCIL

1. Hold a pencil in your left hand, with the pencil point facing toward the left. Let the fingers of your right hand hang over the pencil.

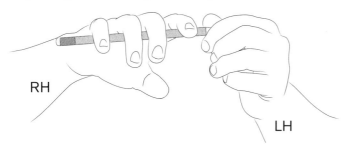

2. Bend and straighten your right thumb several times in the air.

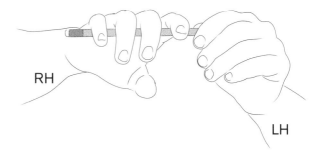

3. Curve or hook your right thumb and place the tip of the thumb on the pencil underneath your right-hand 2nd and 3rd fingers.

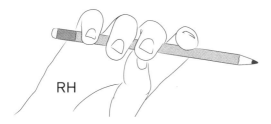

4. Let go with your left hand and rock the pencil back and forth by using your 1st finger and 4th finger.

BASS
SETTING UP THE RIGHT HAND WITH A PENCIL

FRENCH BOW

1. Hold a pencil in your left hand, with the pencil point facing toward the left. Let the fingers of your right hand hang over the pencil.

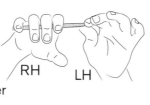

2. Bend and straighten your right thumb several times in the air.

3. Curve or hook your right thumb and place the tip of the thumb on the pencil underneath the space between right-hand 2nd and 3rd fingers.

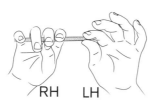

4. Let go with your left hand and rock the pencil back and forth by using your 1st finger and 4th finger.

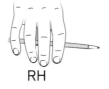

GERMAN BOW

1. Hold a pencil in your left hand, with the pencil point facing toward the left. Place the pencil across the fingers of the right hand.

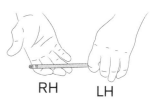

2. Make an "eyeglass" with your right hand thumb and first finger with your palm facing up.

3. Place the pencil in the "eyeglass"

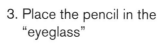

4. Place the your tip of your 2nd and 4th finger under the pencil and let the 3rd finger float in the air.

33

SKIPPING ALONG—*Which notes do not ascend or descend in order like a scale?*

SOUND ADVICE

Ask students to identify the notes that do not move in stepwise motion like a scale.

34 **JINGLE BELLS**—*Listen as you play and identify which lines of music are similar to each other.*

James Lord Pierpont

SOUND ADVICE

Have students listen to the recording and identify which lines are identical and which ones are similar.

42

VIOLIN

SETTING THE RIGHT HAND ON THE BOW

1. Tighten your bow by turning the adjusting screw several turns as instructed by your teacher. Turn the screw clockwise to tighten the bow, and counter-clockwise to loosen it.

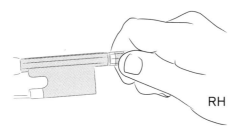

2. Using two hands, pick up the bow in the middle, with the hair facing the floor, and form a good bow hold with your right hand like you did on the pencil. Be careful not to touch the bow hair with your fingers.

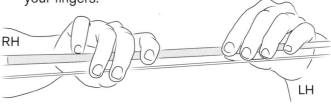

3. Still supporting the bow with your left hand, slide your right hand to the right until the edge of your thumb touches the frog.

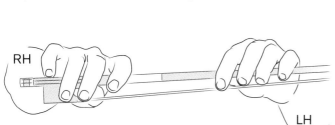

4. Remove your left hand, point the tip of the bow towards the ceiling, and hold the bow with your right hand. Rock it back and forth using your 1st and 4th fingers.

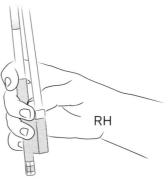

VIOLA

SETTING THE RIGHT HAND ON THE BOW

1. Tighten your bow by turning the adjusting screw several turns as instructed by your teacher. Turn the screw clockwise to tighten the bow, and counter-clockwise to loosen it.

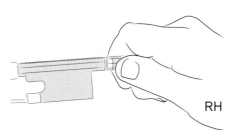

2. Using two hands, pick up the bow in the middle, with the hair facing the floor, and form a good bow hold with your right hand like you did on the pencil. Be careful not to touch the bow hair with your fingers.

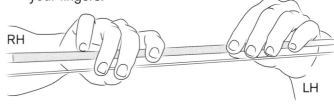

3. Still supporting the bow with your left hand, slide your right hand to the right until the edge of your thumb touches the frog.

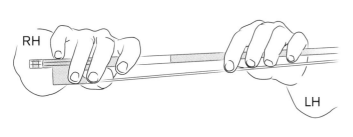

4. Remove your left hand, point the tip of the bow towards the ceiling, and hold the bow with your right hand. Rock it back and forth using your 1st and 4th fingers.

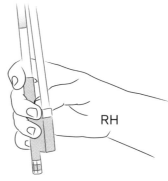

CELLO
SETTING THE RIGHT HAND ON THE BOW

1. Tighten your bow by turning the adjusting screw several turns as instructed by your teacher. Turn the screw clockwise to tighten the bow, and counter-clockwise to loosen it.

2. Using two hands, pick up the bow in the middle, with the hair facing the floor, and form a good bow hold with your right hand like you did on the pencil. Be careful not to touch the bow hair with your fingers.

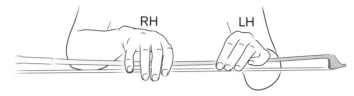

3. Still supporting the bow with your left hand, slide your right hand to the right until the edge of your thumb touches the frog.

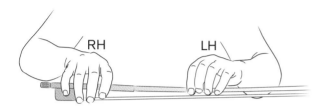

4. Remove your left hand, point the tip of the bow towards the ceiling, and hold the bow with your right hand. Rock it back and forth using your 1st and 4th fingers.

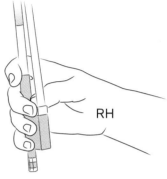

BASS
SETTING UP THE RIGHT HAND ON THE BOW

FRENCH BOW

1. Tighten your bow by turning the screw several turns as instructed by your teacher. Turn the screw clockwise to tighten the bow, and counter-clockwise to loosen it.

2. Using two hands pick up the bow in the middle, with the hair facing the floor and form a good bow hold with your right hand like you did on the pencil.

3. Still supporting the bow with your left hand, slide your right hand to the right until the edge of your thumb touches the frog.

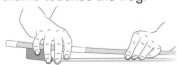

4. Remove your left hand, point the tip of the bow towards the ceiling and hold the bow with your right hand. Rock it back and forth using your 1st and 4th fingers.

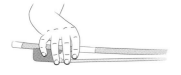

GERMAN BOW

1. Tighten your bow by turning the screw several turns as instructed by your teacher. Turn the screw clockwise to tighten the bow, and counter-clockwise to loosen it.

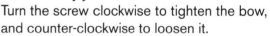

2. Hold the bow in your left hand, with the tip facing toward the left. Still supporting the bow with your left hand, place the bow in the "eyeglass."

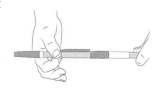

3. Place the tip of your 2nd and 4th fingers under the bow and let the 3rd finger float in the air.

4. Remove your left hand, point the tip of the bow to the left and hold the bow with your right hand.

35   **GOOD KING WENCESLAS**—*Circle the notes that are not on the D string.*

Traditional

SOUND ADVICE

Remind students to relax their shoulders while playing.

36 **DAYENU**—*Practice going from the D string to the A string. D string to G string for basses.*

Hebrew Folk Song

SOUND ADVICE

Remind students to count through the entire last measure before moving.

VIOLIN
MOVING THE BOW **DVD**

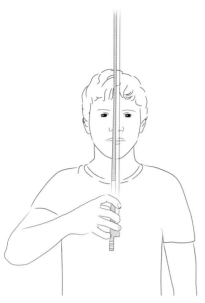
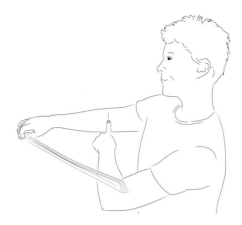
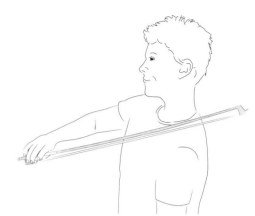

1. Air-Bowing—With the tip pointing toward the ceiling, hold your bow in the air and move it up and down.

2. Place your left-hand 1st finger on the inside of your right elbow. Fold (close) and unfold (open) your right arm.

3. Using a well-formed bow hold, gently pick up the bow and place the tip on your left shoulder. While keeping the bow hair on your shoulder, fold and unfold your right arm.

VIOLA
MOVING THE BOW **DVD**

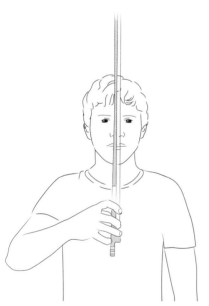
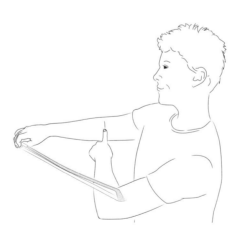
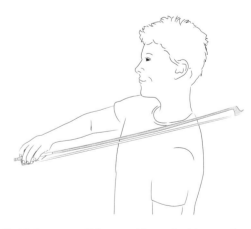

1. Air-Bowing—With the tip pointing toward the ceiling, hold your bow in the air and move it up and down.

2. Place your left-hand 1st finger on the inside of your right elbow. Fold (close) and unfold (open) your right arm.

3. Using a well-formed bow hold, gently pick up the bow and place the tip on your left shoulder. While keeping the bow hair on your shoulder, fold and unfold your right arm.

CELLO
MOVING THE BOW

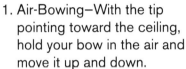

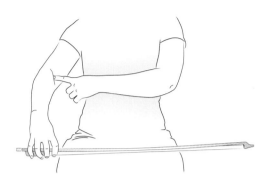

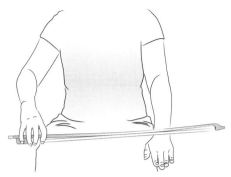

1. Air-Bowing—With the tip pointing toward the ceiling, hold your bow in the air and move it up and down.

2. Place your left-hand 1st finger on the inside of your right elbow. Fold (close) and unfold (open) your right arm.

3. Using a well-formed bow hold, gently pick up the bow and place the bow on your lap behind the cello. While supporting the bow with your left hand, fold and unfold your right arm.

BASS
MOVING THE BOW

FRENCH BOW

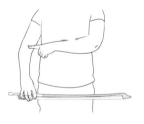

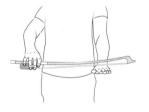

GERMAN BOW

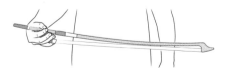

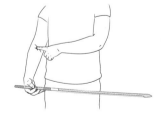

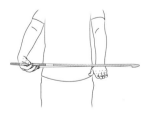

1. Air-Bowing—With the tip pointing toward the left, hold your bow with both hands and move it left and right.

2. Place your left-hand 1st finger on the inside of your right elbow. Fold (close) and unfold (open) your right arm.

3. Using a well-formed bow hold, gently pick up the bow and hold it in front of you in the air. Fold and unforld your right arm.

37 AIR-BOW—*With the tip pointing up (for violins and violas), hold the bow in the air and move it up and down while "air-bowing" the rhythm below. For cellos and basses, move the bow left and right.*

SOUND ADVICE

Remind students to hold the bow in the air in front of their body.

38 AIR-BOW AGAIN—*For violins and violas, move the bow back and forth on your shoulder while "air-bowing" the rhythm below by folding and unfolding your right arm. For cellos and basses, place the bow on your lap.*

SOUND ADVICE

Remind students to place the bow on their shoulder or lap for this exercise.

39   ELLIE'S DANCE—*Continuing to play* pizzicato, *can you make this sound like a dance?*

SOUND ADVICE

Ask students to identify which notes can be removed to create a D descending scale.

40

ANNA'S DANCE—*What is different about the first part of this piece compared to the first part of Ellie's Dance?*

SOUND ADVICE

Ask students to identify the first time a note is skipped in this piece.

41 **CRIPPLE CREEK**—*People often square dance to this piece.*

American Fiddle Tune

SOUND ADVICE

Remind students to keep a steady pulse when playing an energetic piece.

VIOLIN
PLACING THE BOW ON THE STRING 🅓🅥🅓

1. Using a good bow hold at the frog, hold the bow over your head.

2. Set the bow by placing the lower part of the bow on the D string between the end of the fingerboard and the bridge.

3. Lift the bow off the string and then set the middle of the bow on the D string.

4. Lift the bow off the string and then set the upper part of the bow on the D string.

Moving the Bow on the String

ARCO means to play with the bow.

BOW LIFT (ʼ) means to raise the bow off the string and reset it on the string.

DOWN BOW (⊓) means to pull the bow down by moving your hand to the right (away from your body). Just as railroad tracks are parallel to each other, keep the bow parallel to the bridge.

UP BOW (∨) means to push the bow up by moving your hand to the left (toward your body). Remember to keep the bow parallel to the bridge.

VIOLA
PLACING THE BOW ON THE STRING 🅓🅥🅓

1. Using a good bow hold at the frog, hold the bow over your head.

2. Set the bow by placing the lower part of the bow on the D string between the end of the fingerboard and the bridge.

3. Lift the bow off the string and then set the middle of the bow on the D string.

4. Lift the bow off the string and then set the upper part of the bow on the D string.

Moving the Bow on the String

ARCO means to play with the bow.

BOW LIFT (ʼ) means to raise the bow off the string and reset it on the string.

DOWN BOW (⊓) means to pull the bow down by moving your hand to the right (away from your body). Just as railroad tracks are parallel to each other, keep the bow parallel to the bridge.

UP BOW (∨) means to push the bow up by moving your hand to the left (toward your body). Remember to keep the bow parallel to the bridge.

CELLO
PLACING THE BOW ON THE STRING

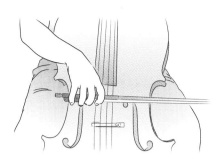

1. Using a good bow hold at the frog, hold the bow over the cello.

2. Set the bow by placing the lower part of the bow on the D string between the end of the fingerboard and the bridge.

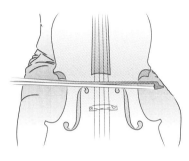

3. Lift the bow off the string and then set the middle of the bow on the D string.

4. Lift the bow off the string and then set the upper part of the bow on the D string.

Moving the Bow on the String

ARCO means to play with the bow.

BOW LIFT (ʼ) means to raise the bow off the string and reset it on the string.

DOWN BOW (⊓) means to pull the bow down by moving your hand to the right (away from your body). Just as railroad tracks are parallel to each other, keep the bow parallel to the bridge.

UP BOW (∨) means to push the bow up by moving your hand to the left (toward your body). Remember to keep the bow parallel to the bridge.

BASS
PLACING THE BOW ON THE STRING

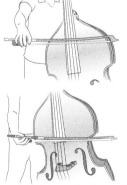

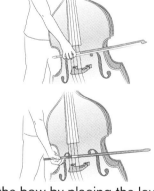

1. Using a good bow hold at the frog, hold the bow over the bass.

2. Set the bow by placing the lower part of the bow on the D string between the end of the fingerboard and the bridge.

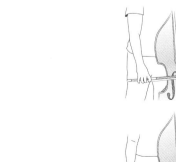

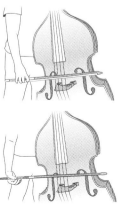

3. Lift the bow off the string and then set the middle of the bow on the D string.

4. Lift the bow off the string and then set the upper part of the bow on the D string.

Moving the Bow on the String

ARCO means to play with the bow.

BOW LIFT (ʼ) means to raise the bow off the string and reset it on the string.

DOWN BOW (⊓) means to pull the bow down by moving your hand to the right (away from your body). Just as railroad tracks are parallel to each other, keep the bow parallel to the bridge.

UP BOW (∨) means to push the bow up by moving your hand to the left (toward your body). Remember to keep the bow parallel to the bridge.

42

BOW THE D STRING—*Play the open D string with the bow. Begin with a down bow as indicated.*

SOUND ADVICE

Remind students to stop the bow before each rest.

43

BOW THE A STRING—*Move your bow to the A string for violins, violas and cellos. Basses move to A on the G string. Play this rhythm.*

SOUND ADVICE

Remind students to play the bowings as marked.

54

44 **D LIFT**—*Practice a bow lift on the D string.*

SOUND ADVICE

Remind students to lift the bow before bar 3.

45 **A LIFT**—*Watch for the bow lift and be sure to play on the A string. G string for basses.*

SOUND ADVICE

Remind the students to place the bow carefully after the lift.

VIOLIN
LEVELS OF THE BOW DVD

Set the bow on top of the bridge on the wood. Gently raise and lower your entire arm to find the different levels that will allow the bow to touch only one string at a time.

String Crossing
Set the bow on top of the bridge at the D-string level. Gently lower your entire arm until the bow crosses over to the A-string level. Now raise your arm until the bow crosses back to the D-string level.

G-string level
Place your bow on the G string.

D-string level
Place your bow on the D string.

A-string level
Place your bow on the A string.

E-string level
Place your bow on the E string.

VIOLA
LEVELS OF THE BOW DVD

Set the bow on top of the bridge on the wood. Gently raise and lower your entire arm to find the different levels that will allow the bow to touch only one string at a time.

String Crossing
Set the bow on top of the bridge at the D-string level. Gently lower your entire arm until the bow crosses over to the A-string level. Now raise your arm until the bow crosses back to the D-string level.

C-string level
Place your bow on the C string.

G-string level
Place your bow on the G string.

D-string level
Place your bow on the D string.

A-string level
Place your bow on the A string.

56

CELLO
LEVELS OF THE BOW

Set the bow on top of the bridge on the wood. Gently raise and lower your entire arm to find the different levels that will allow the bow to touch only one string at a time.

String Crossing
Set the bow on top of the bridge at the D-string level. Gently lower your entire arm until the bow crosses over to the G-string level. Now raise your arm until the bow crosses back to the D-string level.

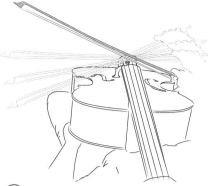

C-string level
Place your bow on the C string.

G-string level
Place your bow on the G string.

D-string level
Place your bow on the D string.

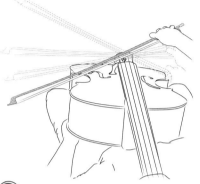

A-string level
Place your bow on the A string.

BASS
LEVELS OF THE BOW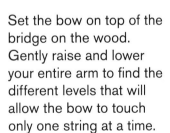

Set the bow on top of the bridge on the wood. Gently raise and lower your entire arm to find the different levels that will allow the bow to touch only one string at a time.

String Crossing
Set the bow on top of the bridge at the D-string level. Gently lower your entire arm until the bow crosses over to the A-string level. Now raise your arm until the bow crosses back to the D-string level.

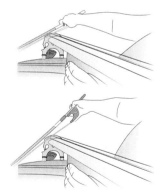

G-string level
Place your bow on the G string.

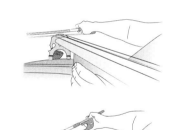

D-string level
Place your bow on the D string.

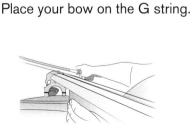

A-string level
Place your bow on the A string.

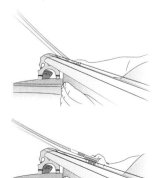

E-string level
Place your bow on the E string.

46

CROSSING OVER D TO A—*Watch the level of your arm as you move from D to A. D to A on the G string for basses.*

SOUND ADVICE

Remind students to change the level of the arm when crossing strings.

47

QUICK CROSS OVER—*Now you have a little less time to change levels.*

SOUND ADVICE

Remind students to change the level of the arm just enough to cross the string.

48 **CHANGING LEVELS**—*Practice changing levels quickly.*

SOUND ADVICE

When crossing strings, remind students to change the level of the arm smoothly.

49 **LIFTS AND LEVELS**—*Watch for bow lifts and the correct arm level. You can do it!*

SOUND ADVICE

Remind students to change the level of the arm while lifting the bow.

VIOLIN

 BOWING LANES are the contact points between the bridge and the fingerboard where the bow is placed. The **CENTER LANE** is halfway between the bridge and the fingerboard. Place your bow on the D string in the center lane. Each time you move your bow, make sure it stays parallel to the bridge and not at an angle.

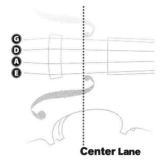

Center Lane

VIOLA

 BOWING LANES are the contact points between the bridge and the fingerboard where the bow is placed. The **CENTER LANE** is halfway between the bridge and the fingerboard. Place your bow on the D string in the center lane. Each time you move your bow, make sure it stays parallel to the bridge and not at an angle.

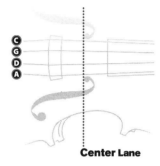

Center Lane

CELLO

 BOWING LANES are the contact points between the bridge and the fingerboard where the bow is placed. The **CENTER LANE** is halfway between the bridge and the fingerboard. Place your bow on the D string in the center lane. Each time you move your bow, make sure it stays parallel to the bridge and not at an angle.

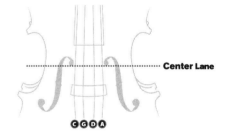

Center Lane

BASS

 BOWING LANES are the contact points between the bridge and the fingerboard where the bow is placed. The **CENTER LANE** is halfway between the bridge and the fingerboard. Place your bow on the D string in the center lane. Each time you move your bow, make sure it stays parallel to the bridge and not at an angle.

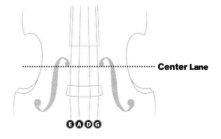

Center Lane

50 **STRAIGHT AS YOU GO**—*Play each of these measures and stop after each one to make sure your bow is parallel to the bridge. Now check the bow of the person next to you.*

SOUND ADVICE

Remind students to stop and make sure the bow is parallel to the bridge.

51 **PARALLEL BOWS**—*Learn to bow D and G. Count silently.*

SOUND ADVICE

Remind students to make sure the bow is parallel to the bridge during down bows and up bows.

52 **BOWING G AND F♯**—*Learn to bow G and F♯. Circle the bow lift.*

SOUND ADVICE

Remind students to make sure the bow is parallel to the bridge during the rests.

53 **FOUR-NOTE TUMBLE**—*Learn to bow G, F♯, E and D.*

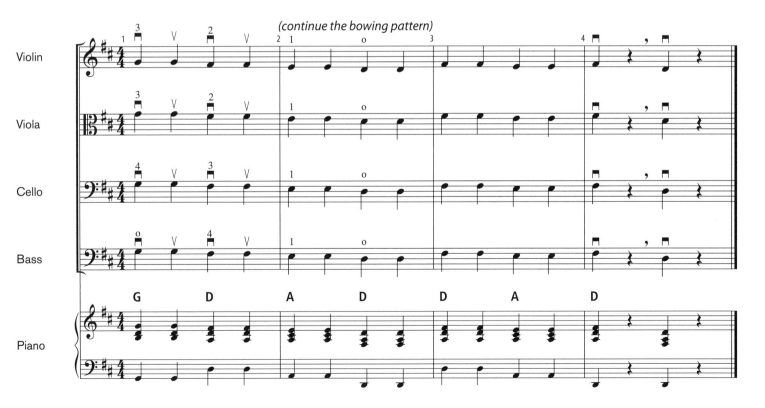

SOUND ADVICE

Remind students to continue the same bowing pattern after bar 1.

54 **MINI SCALE**—*Learn to bow the first half of the D scale.*

SOUND ADVICE

Remind students to watch for the bow lift in the last bar.

55   **MARY HAD A LITTLE LAMB**—*Watch the bow level, the angle to the bridge and the lift.*

Traditional Folk Song

SOUND ADVICE

Have students stop at different times during the piece and check the angle of the bow.

56   **BOWING D AND C♯**—*Learn to bow D and C♯.*

SOUND ADVICE

Remind students to check the angle of the bow during the quarter rests.

57   **FOUR-NOTE RIDE**—*Learn to bow D, C♯, B, and A.*

SOUND ADVICE

Remind students to keep the fingers close to the fingerboard.

58 **WALKING ALONG**—*Practice walking down the A string. G string for basses.*

SOUND ADVICE

Remind students to hold the instruments correctly for a better sound.

59 **LIFTING AS YOU GO**—*Watch for the bow lift.*

SOUND ADVICE

Remind students to place the bow parallel to the bridge after the lifts.

An **INTERVAL** is the distance between two notes.

VIOLIN

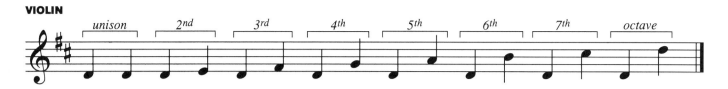

VIOLA

CELLO/BASS

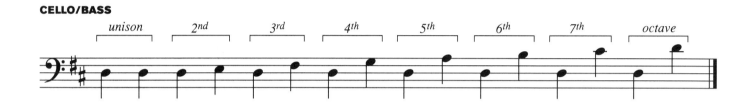

60   **WALKING DOWN THE D SCALE**—*Watch your bow. Is it parallel to the bridge?*

SOUND ADVICE

Have students memorize this scale and then watch their left-hand fingers to make sure they are curved.

61 **WALKING UP THE D SCALE**—*Now we go the other way. What is the interval between the first and last notes of this piece?*

SOUND ADVICE

Have students memorize this scale and watch each other as they play to make sure their stand partner's bow is parallel to the bridge.

62 **PLAYING THE D SCALE**—*Sit up straight, use a good bow hold and watch the placement of your bow. You are doing great!*

SOUND ADVICE

Remind students that the top note in the scale is played twice.

A **HALF NOTE** receives two beats (counts).

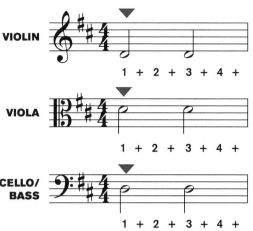

A **HALF REST** receives two beats (counts) of silence.

Half notes can be subdivided into two quarter notes.

Half rests can be subdivided into two quarter rests.

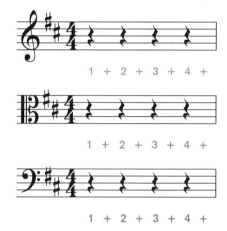

63   **LEARN TO COUNT HALF NOTES AND HALF RESTS**—*Clap, sing and then play the piece.*

SOUND ADVICE

Remind students to clap, sing and then play the piece. Remind them to hold half notes for two beats.

DVD **BOW SPEED** is how fast or slowly the bow moves across the string. Move the bow faster when playing quarter notes and more slowly when playing the half notes.

54 **HOT CROSS BUNS**—*Clap, sing and then play.*

English Folk Song

SOUND ADVICE

Remind students to move the bow more slowly while playing half notes.

65 **ZANDER'S REEL**—*More practice with half notes.*

SOUND ADVICE

Remind students to give the half note in the last bar its full value.

COMPOSITION—*Using quarter notes and/or rests and the pitches D, E, F♯, G and A, fill in each measure to create your own piece of music. This is called composing. Name your piece and then play it when you are finished. Be sure each measure has four beats.*

(Name of piece) _____   Composed by _____

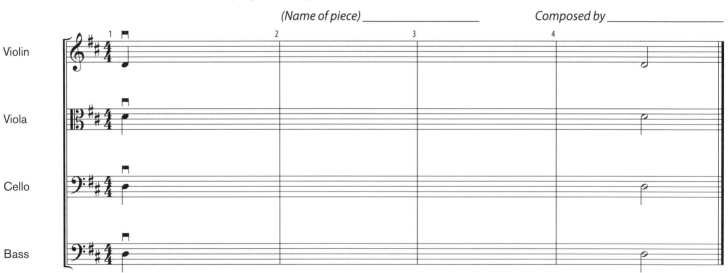

A **RIGHT-FACING REPEAT** shows the first measure of the section to be repeated.

A **LEFT-FACING REPEAT** indicates to go back to the beginning or to the closest right-facing repeat.

1ST AND 2ND ENDINGS: Play the 1st ending the first time through. Repeat the music, but skip over the 1st ending on the repeat and play the 2nd ending instead.

RACHEL'S REPEAT—*Before you play, think about the repeats.*

SOUND ADVICE

Remind students to take the repeats in bars 4 and 8.

67 **LI'L LIZA JANE**—*Be sure to play the 1st and 2nd endings on both lines.*

American Folk Song

SOUND ADVICE

Remind students to skip both first endings after the repeat.

Jacques Offenbach (1819–1880) was a French composer and cellist who wrote operettas in Paris during the Romantic era. One of his best known operettas, *Orpheus in the Underworld*, was written in 1858 just before the beginning of the American Civil War. This operetta contains one of his most famous pieces, *Can-Can*. As a cellist, he performed with pianists Franz Liszt and Felix Mendelssohn, both of whom would later become famous composers themselves.

58

CAN-CAN—*After you have learned* Can-Can, *memorize it. Memorize one measure at a time, gradually adding measures as you go.*

Jacques Offenbach

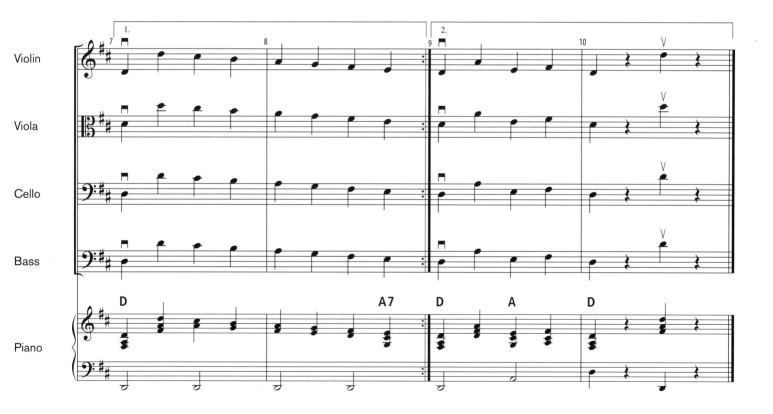

SOUND ADVICE

Have students memorize this piece and then perform it from memory.

An **EIGHTH NOTE** receives a half a beat (count) in $\frac{4}{4}$ time. Two eighth notes equal one beat in $\frac{4}{4}$ time. Eighth notes often appear in pairs or fours and have a *beam* across the note stems.

A quarter note can be subdivided into two eighth notes.

Four quarter notes can be subdivided into eight eighth notes.

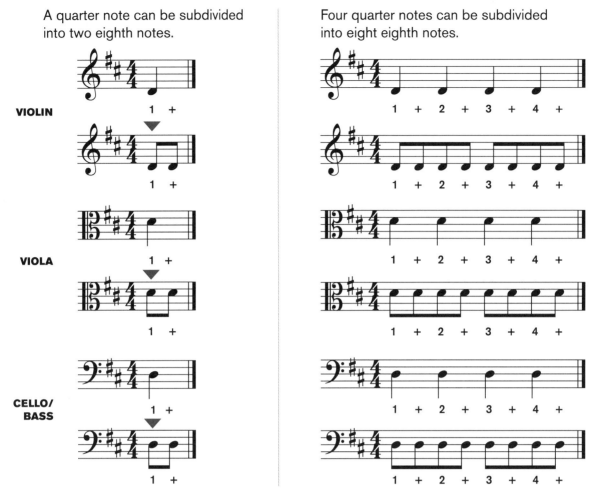

69   **COUNTING QUARTER NOTES AND EIGHTH NOTES**—*Clap while counting aloud.*
Next, sing and then play the piece.

SOUND ADVICE

Remind students to fold and unfold the elbow when playing eighth notes.

COUNTING QUARTER NOTES, EIGHTH NOTES AND HALF NOTES
— *Clap while counting aloud. Next, sing and then play the piece.*

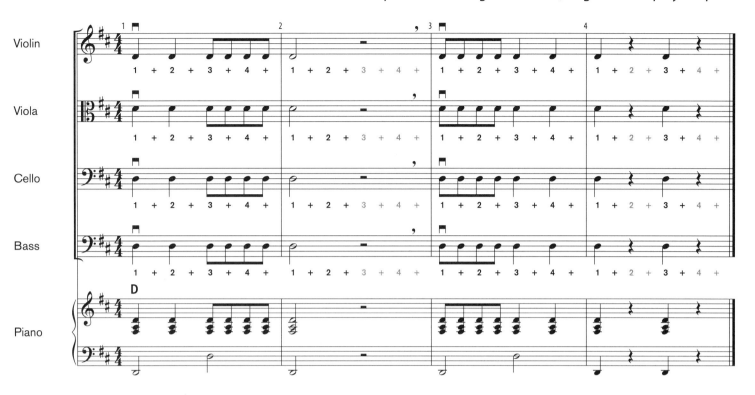

SOUND ADVICE

Remind students to slow the bow down when going from eighth notes to half notes or quarter notes.

DOUBLETIME—*Play the D scale with pairs of eighth notes.*

SOUND ADVICE

Remind students to play in the middle of the bow when playing eighth notes.

72   **OATS, PEAS AND BEANS**—*Write in the counting numbers on the lines.*

Traditional Folk Song

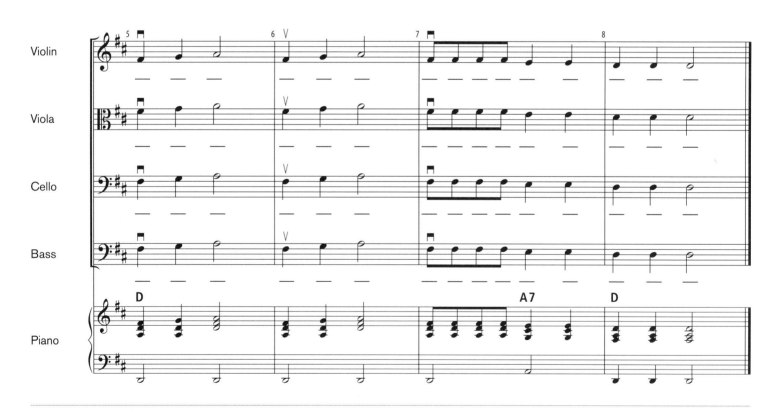

SOUND ADVICE

Have students check each other's written-in counting numbers.

SOUND CHECK Check off each skill you have mastered.

___ Playing position   ___ Bowing levels
___ Bow hold   ___ Counting quarter, half, and eighth notes
___ Left-hand placement   ___ Play the D scale

Level 2: Sound Fundamentals

LEFT-HAND PIZZICATO (+) tells you to pluck the string with the 4ᵗʰ finger of the left hand.

73

FINGER PLUCKS—*Play arco and then pluck with the 4th finger.*

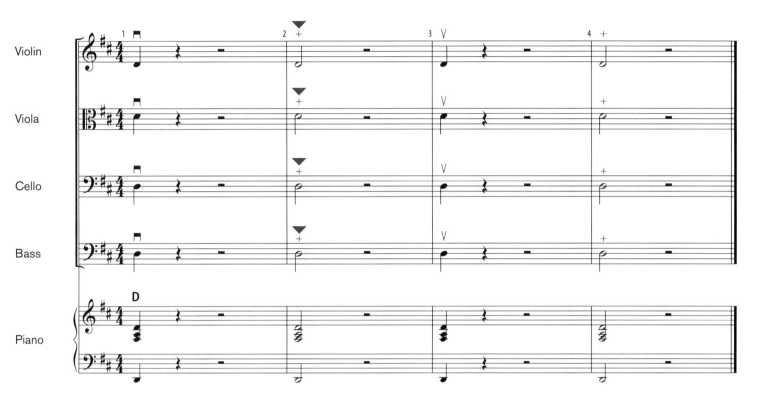

SOUND ADVICE

Remind students to pull the D string forcefully with the 4ᵗʰ finger.

NEW NOTE

A

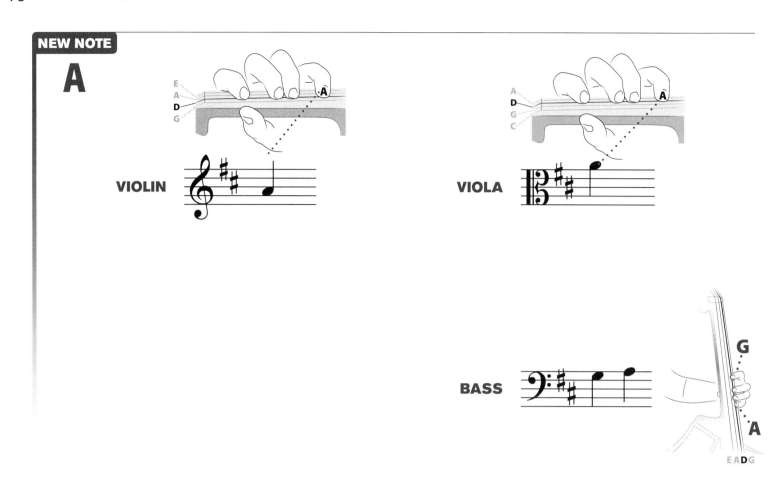

VIOLIN

VIOLA

BASS

74   **FOURTH FINGER A ON THE D STRING**—*Violins and violas, make sure your 4th finger is in tune by comparing it to the open A. Cellos play open A. Basses learn to play G and A on the D string.*

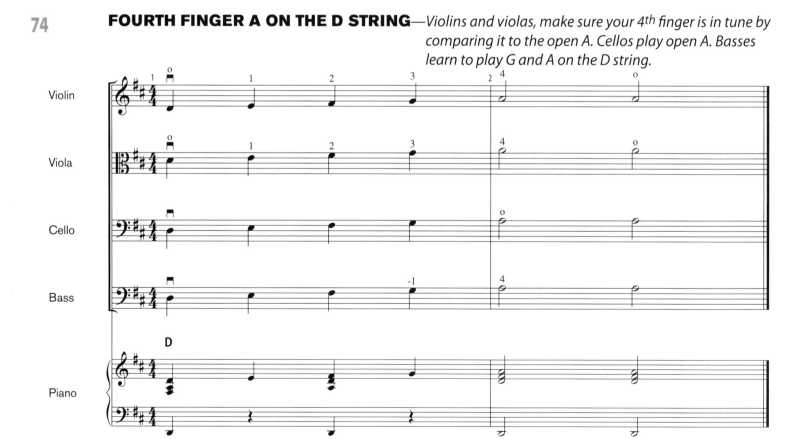

SOUND ADVICE

Remind violins and violas to compare their 4th finger A to the open A string. Basses learn to finger G and A in 3rd position on the D string. Remind students to watch the DVD to review tips on finger placement.

75 **A NEW WAY TO PLAY A**—*Violins and violas play A with the 4th finger. Cellos use open A. Basses play A with the 4th finger.*

SOUND ADVICE

Point out to violins and violas that the 4th finger will create a tunnel over the A string. Remind basses to shift back to first position during the rest.

76 **FRÈRE JACQUES**—*In this familiar song we practice repeats and the 4th-finger A for violins, violas and basses. Cellos use open A.*

French Folk Song

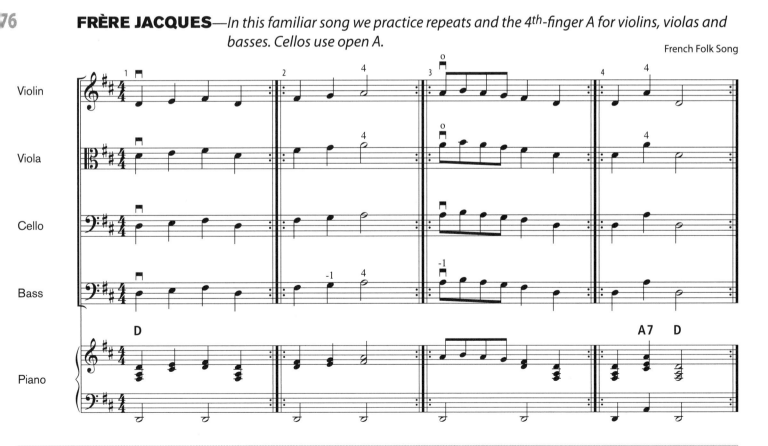

SOUND ADVICE

After students learn to play the tune, have them play it as a round.

77 **DREYDL, DREYDL**—*How many times do you play an A?*

Jewish Folk Song

SOUND ADVICE

Remind students to look for fingerings above the music.

78

SHEPHERD'S HEY—*Play the left-hand pizzicato notes with emphasis.*

English-Australian Folk Song

SOUND ADVICE

Remind students to play 4th finger pizzicatos with force in the left hand.

VIOLIN/VIOLA

USING DIFFERENT PARTS OF THE BOW

The whole bow can be divided into three parts:
the *lower* half (from the frog to the middle),
the *upper* half (from the middle to the tip) and
the *middle*, which overlaps the upper and lower parts.

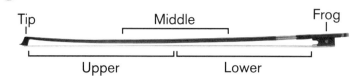

Play in the lower half by starting at the frog and moving to the middle.

Play in the upper half by starting at the middle and moving to the tip.

Play a whole bow by starting at the frog and moving to the tip.

Play in the middle by starting near the middle and moving just past the middle.

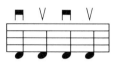

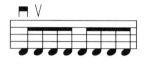

CELLO

USING DIFFERENT PARTS OF THE BOW

The whole bow can be divided into three parts:
the *lower* half (from the frog to the middle),
the *upper* half (from the middle to the tip) and
the *middle*, which overlaps the upper and lower parts.

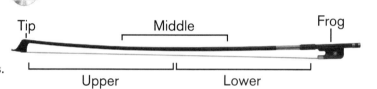

Play in the lower half by starting at the frog and moving to the middle.

Play in the upper half by starting at the middle and moving to the tip.

Play a whole bow by starting at the frog and moving to the tip.

Play in the middle by starting near the middle and moving just past the middle.

BASS

USING DIFFERENT PARTS OF THE BOW

The whole bow can be divided into three parts:
the *lower* half (from the frog to the middle),
the *upper* half (from the middle to the tip) and
the *middle*, which overlaps the upper and lower parts.

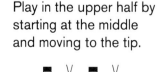

Play in the lower half by starting at the frog and moving to the middle.

Play in the upper half by starting at the middle and moving to the tip.

Play a whole bow by starting at the frog and moving to the tip.

Play in the middle by starting near the middle and moving just past the middle.

79 **UP ON THE HOUSETOP**—*Play in the upper half of the bow.*

Benjamin Hanby

SOUND ADVICE

Remind students that a good tone starts with good posture and playing position.

80

VIOLIN

A New Time Signature

2 = Two beats (counts) to a measure.
4 = A quarter note receives one beat (count).

RHYTHMS IN 2/4—*Clap while counting aloud. Next, sing and then play the piece.*

1 + 2 +   1 + 2 +   1 + 2 +   1 + 2 +

VIOLA

A New Time Signature

2 = Two beats (counts) to a measure.
4 = A quarter note receives one beat (count).

RHYTHMS IN 2/4—*Clap while counting aloud. Next, sing and then play the piece.*

1 + 2 +   1 + 2 +   1 + 2 +   1 + 2 +

CELLO/BASS

A New Time Signature

2 = Two beats (counts) to a measure.
4 = A quarter note receives one beat (count).

RHYTHMS IN 2/4—*Clap while counting aloud. Next, sing and then play the piece.*

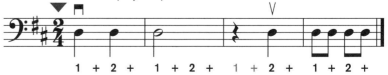

1 + 2 +   1 + 2 +   1 + 2 +   1 + 2 +

SOUND ADVICE

Remind students that counting numbers in gray indicate a rest. Remind the students to notice the new time signature.

81   **LUZ DE LA MAÑANA**—*Play in the middle part of the bow.*

Latin Folk Song

SOUND ADVICE

Have students set the bow at the frog, at the tip and in the middle. Then perform the piece in the middle of the bow.

A **ROUND** is a type of music in which players start the piece at different times, creating interesting harmonies and accompaniments. After the first player has played one measure of *Reuben and Rachel*, the second player begins the song. Listen to see if you're playing together and are in tune with each other.

32 **DVD** **REUBEN AND RACHEL**—*Play in the lower part of the bow. Play the piece again using the upper part of the bow. How does this change the sound?*

William Gooch

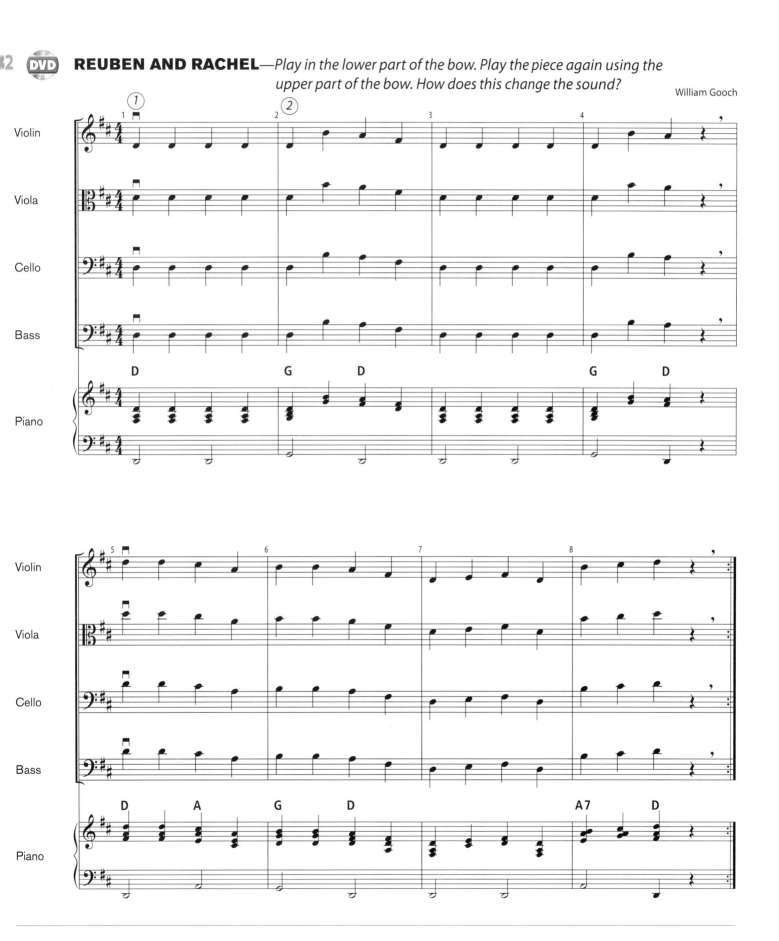

SOUND ADVICE

This piece can be performed as a round. Assign students to either part 1 or 2 and then perform the piece.

86

TEMPO MARKINGS indicate how fast or slow the music should be played.

ANDANTE is a slow tempo.   **MODERATO** is a moderate tempo.   **ALLEGRO** is a fast tempo.

A **DUET** is a composition for two performers. When both parts are played together, you will hear two notes played at the same time, which creates **HARMONY**.

83

LIGHTLY ROW—*Your teacher will tell you which part to play. Switch parts on the repeat.*

SOUND ADVICE

Remind students to switch parts on the repeat. The soloist on the Accompaniment CD plays part A the first time through and part B the second time. Students can play a duet with the recording by playing part B the first time and part A the second time. Remind students to watch for tempo markings.

THIS OLD MAN—*While playing this duet, remember to change string levels by moving your right arm to the correct level of the bow for each string. Switch parts on the repeat.*

American Folk Song

SOUND ADVICE

Remind students that they can play a duet with the recording by playing part B the first time and part A the second time.

A New Time Signature

3 = Three beats (counts) to a measure.

4 = A quarter note receives one beat (count).

A **DOT** increases the length of a note by half its value.
A **DOTTED HALF NOTE** receives three beats (counts) and can be subdivided into three quarter notes.

85   **RHYTHMS IN 3/4** —*Clap while counting aloud. Next, sing and then play the piece.*

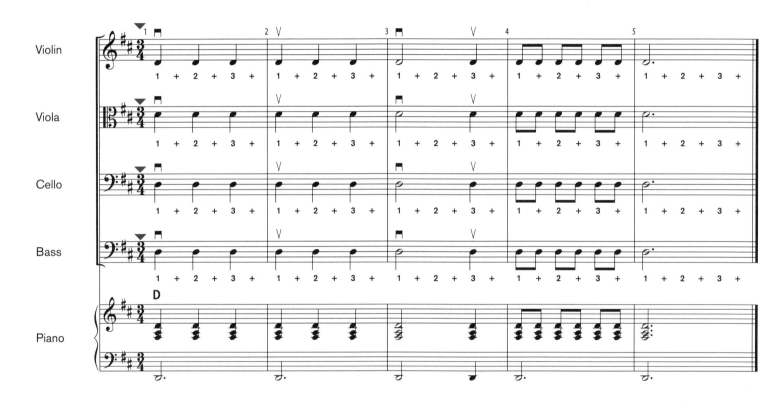

SOUND ADVICE

Have half the students clap the rhythm of the tune while the other half plays, then reverse. Remind students to notice the new time signature.

VIOLIN

A **CHORD** is three or more notes played at the same time. This creates harmony.

An **ARPEGGIO** is the notes of a chord played one after another.

D MAJOR ARPEGGIO

VIOLA

A **CHORD** is three or more notes played at the same time. This creates harmony.

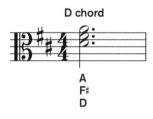

An **ARPEGGIO** is the notes of a chord played one after another.

D MAJOR ARPEGGIO

CELLO/BASS

A **CHORD** is three or more notes played at the same time. This creates harmony.

An **ARPEGGIO** is the notes of a chord played one after another.

D MAJOR ARPEGGIO

86 **SCALING IN THREE**—*Play the D Major scale and arpeggio in 3/4 time.*

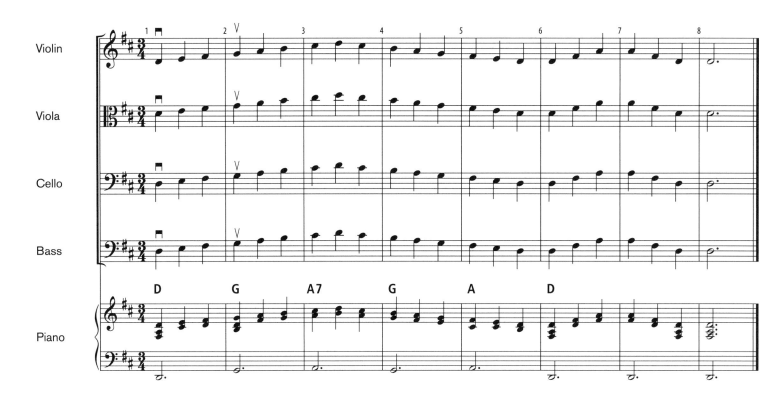

SOUND ADVICE

Ask students to identify which bars contain scale patterns and which contain arpeggio patterns.

87 **LAVENDER'S BLUE**—*Before playing, think through the repeat and endings.*

SOUND ADVICE

Remind students to hold the dotted half notes for 3 beats.

FRENCH FOLK SONG—*Practice playing in $\frac{3}{4}$ time.*

Traditional

SOUND ADVICE

Remind students to play in a relaxed manner. Watch for raised or tense shoulders. Remind basses to watch the DVD to review tips on finger placement.

Placing Fingers on the G String (A & E STRING FOR BASSES) DVD

VIOLIN

The new key signature of **G MAJOR** tells you that all F's are to be played sharp.

Reminder: **LEDGER LINES** are short, horizontal lines used to extend a staff either higher or lower.

VIOLA

The new key signature of **G MAJOR** tells you that all F's are to be played sharp.

Reminder: **LEDGER LINES** are short, horizontal lines used to extend a staff either higher or lower.

CELLO/BASS

The new key signature of **G MAJOR** tells you that all F's are to be played sharp.

Reminder: **LEDGER LINES** are short, horizontal lines used to extend a staff either higher or lower.

NEW NOTE

G

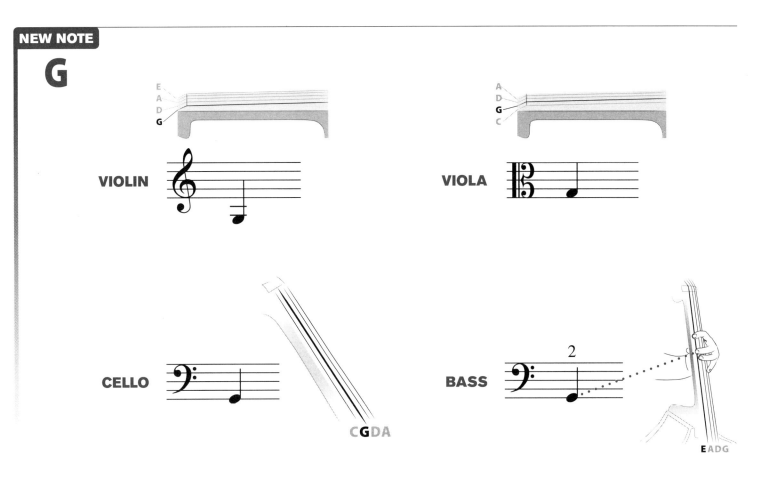

VIOLIN

VIOLA

CELLO

BASS

NEW NOTE OPEN G STRING—*Learn to play the open G string for violins, violas and cellos. Basses play G on the E string.*

SOUND ADVICE

When moving to the G string, make sure violins and violas raise the right arm while cellos and basses lower the right arm. Basses are playing G on the E string. Remind students to watch the DVD to review tips on finger placement.

NEW NOTE

C

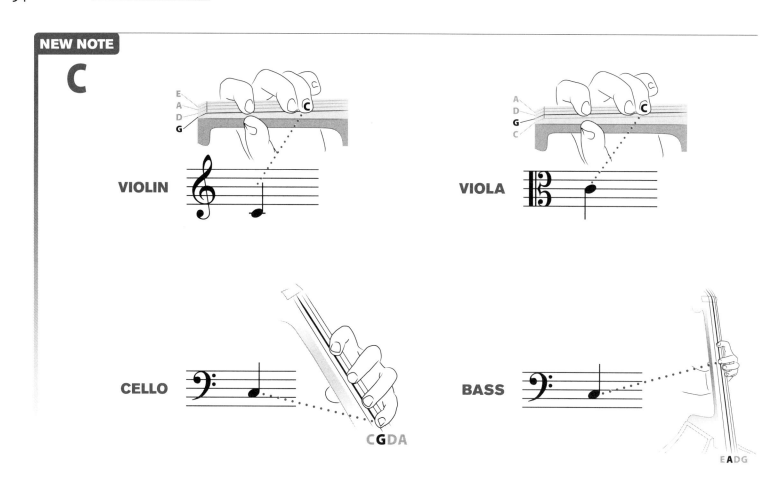

VIOLIN

VIOLA

CELLO

C G D A

BASS

E A D G

90   **NEW NOTE C**—*Learn to play C on the G string for violins, violas and cellos.*
        Basses learn to play C on the A string.

SOUND ADVICE

Remind violins and violas to bring the left elbow under the neck when placing fingers on the G string.

C AND G JUMPS—*Learn to move between C and G.*

SOUND ADVICE

Remind students to leave the fingers close to the fingerboard while playing the open G string.

NEW NOTE

B

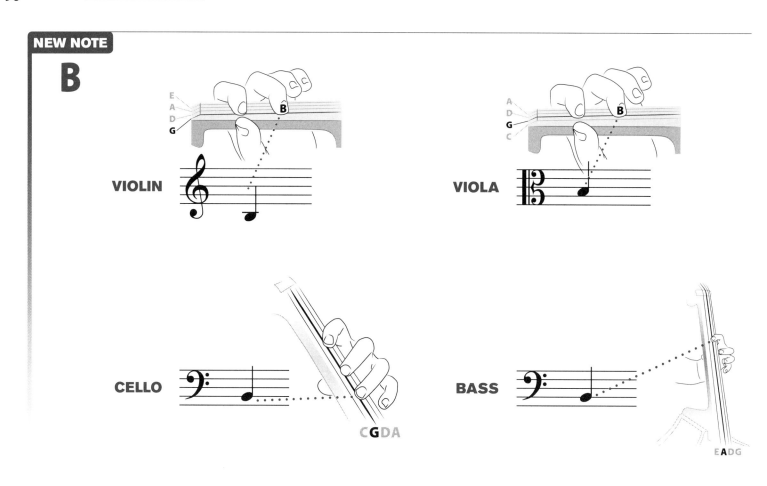

VIOLIN

VIOLA

CELLO

BASS

92   **NEW NOTE B**—*Learn to play B on the G string for violins, violas and cellos. Basses play B on the A string.*

Violin

Viola

Cello

Bass

Piano

SOUND ADVICE

Remind students to relax the left-hand thumb while playing B.

B AND G JUMPS—*Learn to move between B and G.*

SOUND ADVICE

Remind students to keep the left wrist straight and not to let it cave in.

NEW NOTE

A

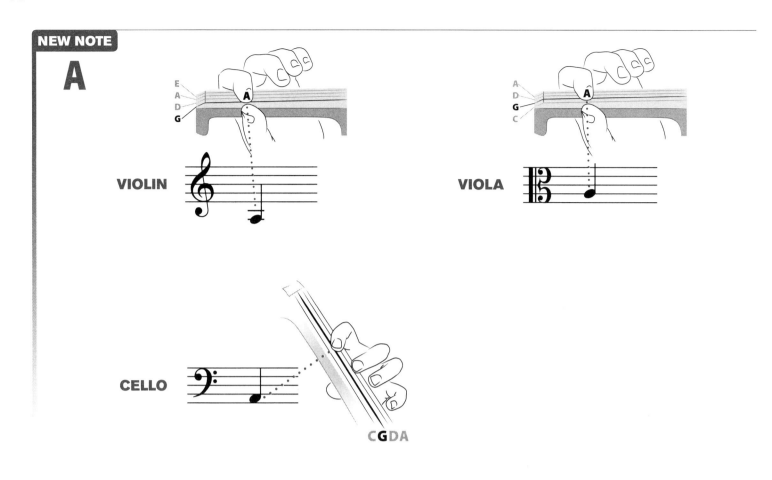

VIOLIN

VIOLA

CELLO

94   **NEW NOTE A**—*Learn to play A on the G string. Basses review.*

SOUND ADVICE

Basses will review the open A string, while violins, violas and cellos learn to play A on the G string.

A AND G JUMPS—*Learn to move between A and G.*

SOUND ADVICE

Remind the basses that they will have to cross strings while going from open A to G on the E string.

GOIN' LOW—*Practice walking down and then up the G string. A and E for basses. What is the key signature?*

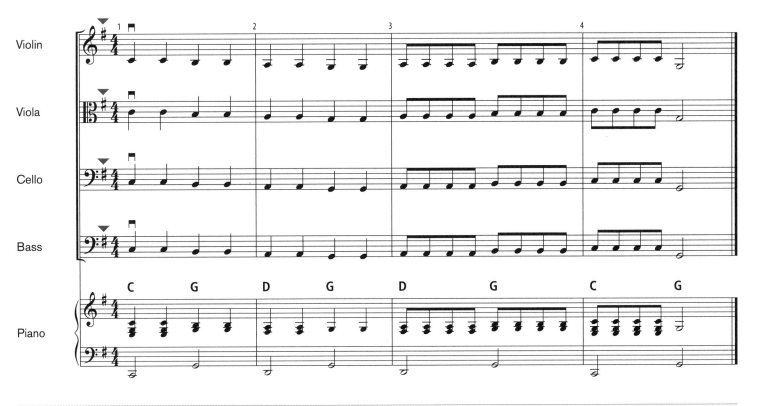

SOUND ADVICE

Remind students to place the left-hand fingers firmly on the string.

97   GOING UP THE LINE—*Play on the G string in ¾ time. E, A and D strings for basses.*

SOUND ADVICE

Remind students to practice with the Accompaniment CD.

98   G MAJOR SCALE—*Before playing, write the name of each note on the line. Check your string level by watching your arm.*

SOUND ADVICE

Remind students to watch the arm level when crossing strings.

G MAJOR ARPEGGIO—*This is similar to the D arpeggio, but it starts on G.*

SOUND ADVICE

Remind violins and violas to keep the instrument parallel to the floor.

NEW NOTE

D

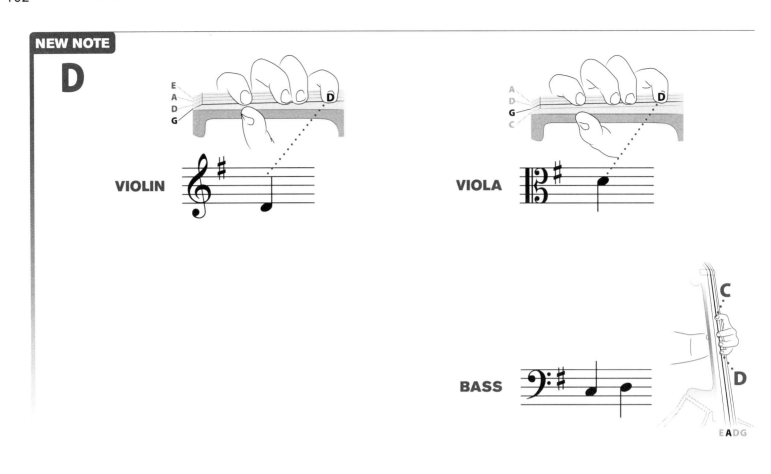

VIOLIN

VIOLA

BASS

100 (DVD) **A NEW WAY TO PLAY D**—*Learn to play D with the 4th finger on the G string for violins and violas. Cellos play the open D string. Basses learn C and D with the 4th finger on the A string.*

SOUND ADVICE

Demonstrate checking the 4th finger D with the open D string to find out if it is in tune. Cellos review. Remind students to watch the DVD to review the placement of fingers.

D.C. AL FINE–Go back to the beginning and play through to the **FINE** (the end).

A **DOUBLE BAR LINE** indicates the end of a section.

GO TELL AUNT RHODY—*Remember to go back to the beginning and play to the* Fine.

SOUND ADVICE

Have students point to the *D.C. al Fine*, the beginning, and the *Fine* before playing.

VIOLIN

A **TIE** is a curved line that connects two or more notes of the same pitch. The tied notes are played as one longer note with the combined value of both notes.

VIOLA

A **TIE** is a curved line that connects two or more notes of the same pitch. The tied notes are played as one longer note with the combined value of both notes.

CELLO/BASS

A **TIE** is a curved line that connects two or more notes of the same pitch. The tied notes are played as one longer note with the combined value of both notes.

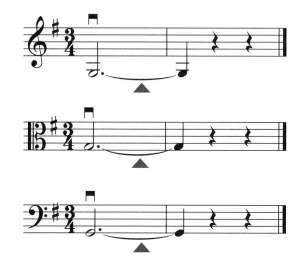

102

BARCAROLLE—*What is the time signature of this piece? Be sure to count the beats of the tied notes.*

Jacques Offenbach

SOUND ADVICE

Remind students to hold the tied notes for the full value.

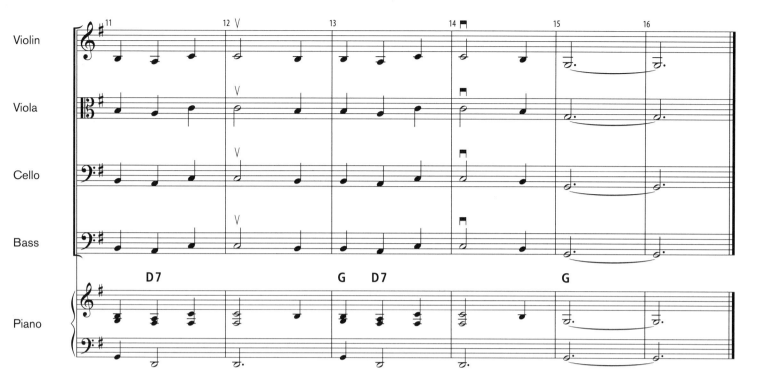

VIOLIN

A **PICKUP** is a note (or notes) that occurs before the first complete measure of a piece. Often the last measure of the piece will be missing the same number of beats as the pickup notes have.

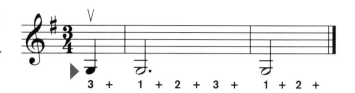

A **STACCATO** mark (·) placed above or below a note indicates that it should be played short and detached. Separate the notes by stopping the bow.

A **TENUTO** (legato) mark (−) placed above or below a note indicates that it should be held for its full value and played smoothly.

VIOLA

A **PICKUP** is a note (or notes) that occurs before the first complete measure of a piece. Often the last measure of the piece will be missing the same number of beats as the pickup notes have.

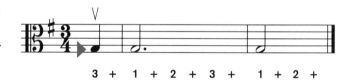

A **STACCATO** mark (·) placed above or below a note indicates that it should be played short and detached. Separate the notes by stopping the bow.

A **TENUTO** (legato) mark (−) placed above or below a note indicates that it should be held for its full value and played smoothly.

CELLO/BASS

A **PICKUP** is a note (or notes) that occurs before the first complete measure of a piece. Often the last measure of the piece will be missing the same number of beats as the pickup notes have.

A **STACCATO** mark (·) placed above or below a note indicates that it should be played short and detached. Separate the notes by stopping the bow.

A **TENUTO** (legato) mark (−) placed above or below a note indicates that it should be held for its full value and played smoothly.

3

BUFFALO GALS—*Play this piece staccato and tenuto where marked, and be sure to count carefully so the half notes receive their full value. How many beats are in the pickup? How many beats are missing from the last measure?*

American Folk Song

SOUND ADVICE

Remind students to stop the bow after each staccato note and move the bow smoothly while playing legato notes. Remind students to notice the tied notes.

NEW NOTE FOR BASSES

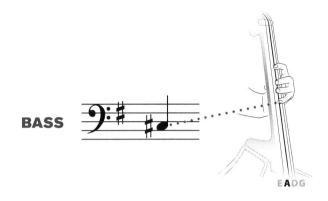

BASS

104 **NEW NOTE C♯ FOR BASSES**—*Basses learn to play 4th finger C♯ on the A string.*
Violins, violas and cellos review.

SOUND ADVICE

Remind basses to open up the left hand while playing the new note C♯ on the A string. Remind basses to watch the DVD to review tips on finger placement.

VIOLIN

A **SLUR** is a curved line placed above or below two or more different notes. It tells you to play the notes smoothly in the same bow direction.

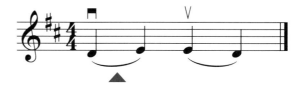

 VIOLA

A **SLUR** is a curved line placed above or below two or more different notes. It tells you to play the notes smoothly in the same bow direction.

 CELLO/BASS

A **SLUR** is a curved line placed above or below two or more different notes. It tells you to play the notes smoothly in the same bow direction.

5 **CONNECTABLE**—*Practice slurring between D and E.*

SOUND ADVICE

Remind students to keep the bow moving through the entire slur. Watch the DVD to review tips about playing slurs.

106   CONNECTABLE ON D—*Play the notes on the D string with the slurs as marked. D and G strings for bass.*

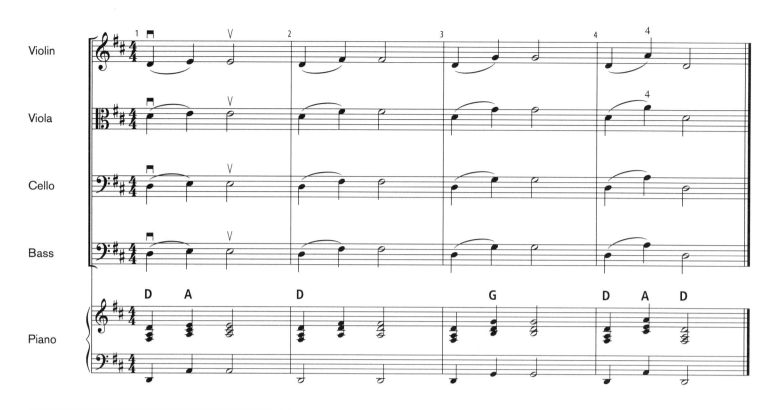

SOUND ADVICE

Point out to students that the bow is moving in half-note rhythms even when playing the slurred quarter notes.

107   CONNECTABILITY UP AND DOWN—*Play the D scale with slurs.*

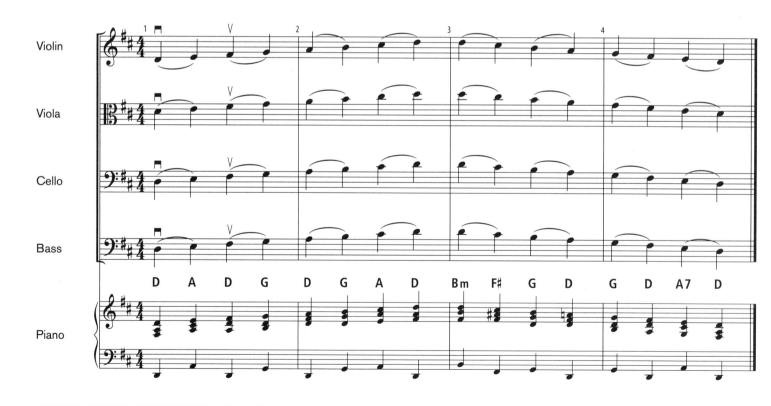

SOUND ADVICE

Remind students to move the bow at the same speed when playing both down bows and up bows.

VIOLIN
 HOOKED BOWING
A curved line above or below two notes with staccato marks tells you to play the notes with stops in the same bow direction.

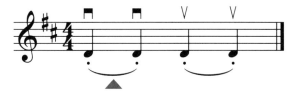

VIOLA
 HOOKED BOWING
A curved line above or below two notes with staccato marks tells you to play the notes with stops in the same bow direction.

CELLO/BASS
 HOOKED BOWING
A curved line above or below two notes with staccato marks tells you to play the notes with stops in the same bow direction.

HOOK THE BOW—*Practice stopping the bow and continuing in the same direction.*

SOUND ADVICE

Remind students to leave the bow in the same place on the string while counting the rests. Watch the DVD to review tips about playing hooked bowings.

109 **SLURS AND HOOKS ON THE D SCALE**—*Play the D scale and watch carefully for the slurs and hooks.*

SOUND ADVICE

Remind students to use an equal amount of bow whether playing quarter note slurs or hooks.

113

MINUET NO. 1—*Discuss with your teacher the characteristics of music written during this period in music history. Listen to the recording of this piece and describe those characteristics.*

Johann Sebastian Bach

SOUND ADVICE

Remind students to move the bow quickly on the first beat of bar one and more slowly on the quarter-note hooks.

COMMON TIME (C) indicates the $\frac{4}{4}$ time signature.

A **HALF STEP** is the smallest distance between two notes.

A **WHOLE STEP** is a whole tone or two half steps.

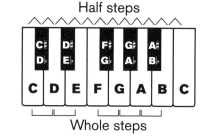

Half steps

Whole steps

VIOLIN

VIOLA

CELLO/BASS

111 **D MAJOR SCALE WITH WHOLE STEPS AND HALF STEPS**—*All major scales use the same pattern of whole steps and half steps.*

SOUND ADVICE

Have students evaluate their stand partner's playing position while playing the D scale.

2 **STRING SLURS**—*While playing with a slurred bowing, practice crossing to a different string.*

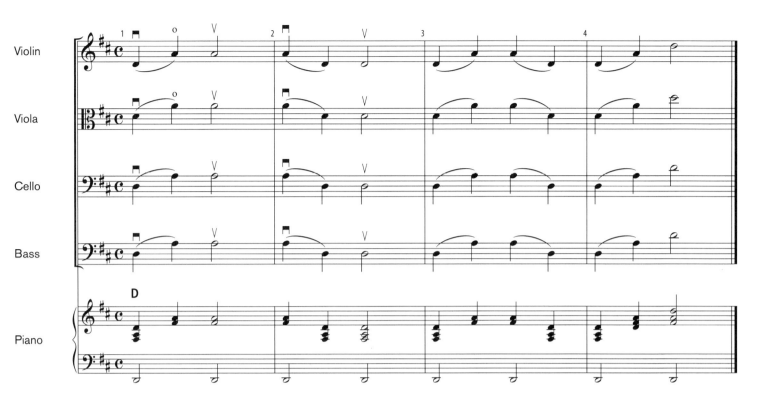

SOUND ADVICE

Remind students to raise or lower the left arm smoothly when slurring across strings.

13 **MORE STRING SLURS**—*Practice staying close to both strings when crossing.*

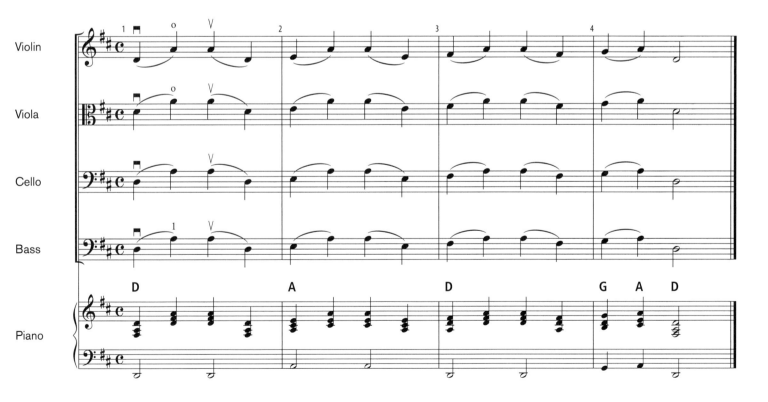

SOUND ADVICE

Remind students to keep the left-hand fingers down through the entire bar in measures 2 and 3.

116

A **CONCERTO** is a composition for orchestra and soloist. Beethoven wrote his violin concerto in 1806.

114 **THEME FROM VIOLIN CONCERTO**—*Watch carefully for the slurred eighth notes.*

Ludwig van Beethoven

SOUND ADVICE

Have students perform this piece standing and remind them how to place their feet.

115 **SWEET BETSY FROM PIKE**—*Watch carefully for the slurred string crossings.*

American Folk Song

SOUND ADVICE

Remind students to check the tempo marking before playing the piece.

A **NATURAL** (♮) cancels a **SHARP** (♯) or **FLAT** (♭) and lasts until the end of the measure.
Reminder: an **ACCIDENTAL** is a sharp, flat or natural sign used to raise, lower or return a note to its
normal pitch. The effect lasts until the end of the measure. You will learn more about flats in Book 2.

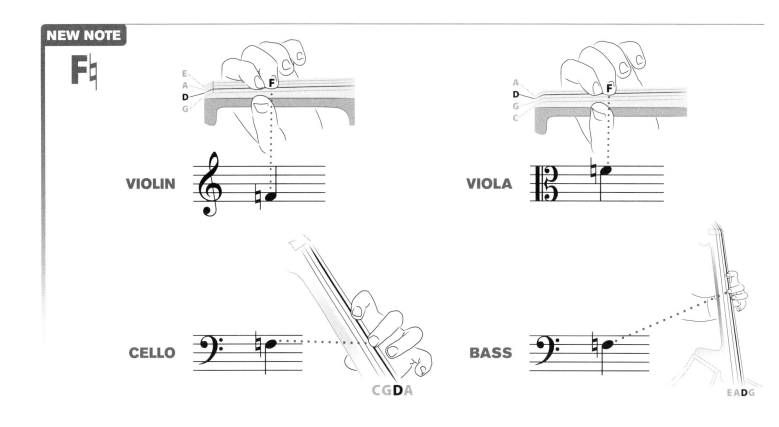

116 **DVD** **NEW NOTE F♮**—*Violins and violas learn to play low 2nd finger (Lo 2). Cellos and basses learn to play 2nd finger on the D string.*

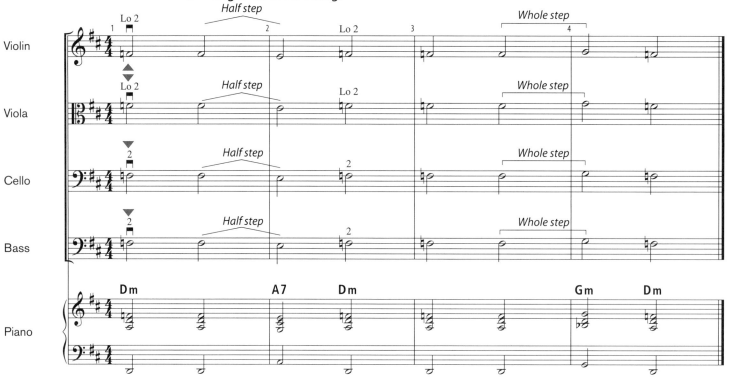

SOUND ADVICE

Remind students to watch the DVD to review tips on finger placement. Remind them that accidentals last through the entire bar.

7 PLAYING AROUND F♮—*Learn to play F♮ on the D string.*

SOUND ADVICE

Make sure violins and violas do not bring the left-hand 3rd finger back when playing F natural. Remind basses to maintain a half-step space between the left-hand 1st finger and 2nd finger.

8 PLAYING F♯ AND F♮—*Violins and violas can play 2nd finger either high (Hi 2) or low (Lo 2). Cellos play 2nd and 3rd fingers. Basses play 2nd and 4th fingers.*

SOUND ADVICE

Have violins and violas hold the left hand up and demonstrate the Hi 2 finger pattern and then the Lo 2 finger pattern.

119 **HI-LO**—*Moving the 2nd finger for violins and violas. Cellos play 2nd and 3rd fingers. Basses play 2nd and 4th fingers.*

SOUND ADVICE

Have violins and violas hold the left hand up and practice sliding the 2nd finger from Hi 2 to Lo 2 and back again.

120 **FINGER ROCK**—*Go from F♮ to F♯.*

SOUND ADVICE

Remind students to completely depress the finger on the string before making a sound.

NEW NOTE

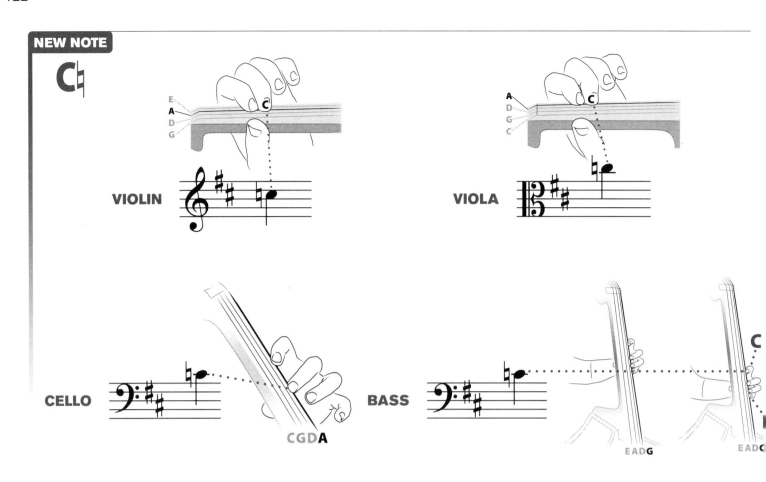

121 (DVD) **NEW NOTE C♮**—*Learn to play low 2nd finger (Lo 2) for violins and Violas. Cellos play 2nd finger on the A string. Basses play on the G string.*

SOUND ADVICE

Remind students to watch the DVD to review tips on finger placement. Basses will learn to play C♮ on the G string in 2nd and 3rd position.

2 **PLAYING AROUND C♮**—*Learn to play C♮ on the A string. G string for basses.*

SOUND ADVICE

Remind violins and violas to keep the third finger above the string while playing Lo 2 or Hi 2.

3 **LO-HI**—*Moving the 2nd finger for violins and violas. Cellos play C♮ and C♯ on the A string. G string for basses.*

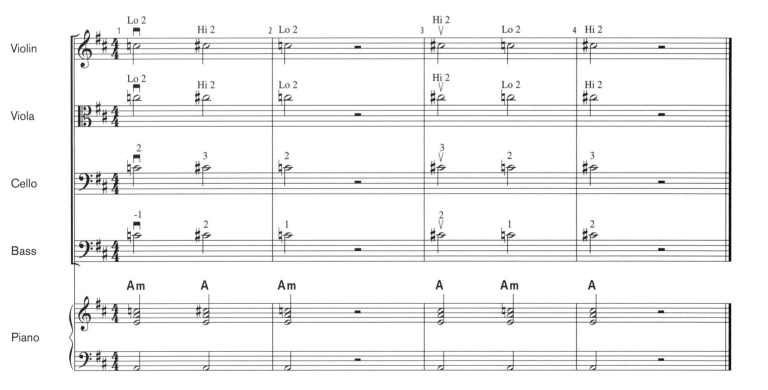

SOUND ADVICE

Remind violins and violas to move from Lo 2 to Hi 2 as they are changing bow direction.

124

ODE TO JOY ON THE A STRING—*Play* Ode To Joy *using C♮.*

Ludwig van Beethoven

SOUND ADVICE

Remind students to change bow directions as smoothly as possible.

5 **PLAYING C♮**—*Playing Lo 2 and Hi 2 in the same piece for violins and violas. Playing C♮ using 2nd and 3rd fingers for cellos. Playing C♮ using 1st and 4th fingers for basses.*

SOUND ADVICE

Remind students to make sure the left-hand thumb is bent.

126   **THE MINSTREL BOY**—*Playing both F♮ and C♮.*

Irish Folk Song

SOUND ADVICE

Remind students to play smoothly with a connected bow.

SOUND CHECK
Check off each skill you have mastered.

___ Correct bow division   ___ Playing staccato and tenuto

___ Playing in different tempos   ___ Playing slurred and hooked bowing

___ Reading G-string notes   ___ Playing C natural and F natural

Level 3: Sound Musicianship

The new key signature of **C MAJOR** indicates that there are no sharps or flats and all notes are natural.

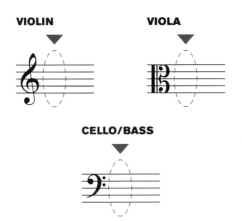

DYNAMICS are changes in volume. We use symbols to indicate how loud or soft to play.

MEZZO FORTE (*mf*) indicates to play medium loud. Do this by placing your bow in the mezzo forte (center) lane. Use a medium amount of arm weight and a medium-fast bow speed.

FORTE (*f*) indicates to play loudly. Do this by placing your bow in the forte lane. Use more arm weight and a slower bow speed.

PIANO (*p*) indicates to play softly. Do this by placing your bow in the piano lane. Use less arm weight and a faster bow speed.

VIOLIN

A **BOWING LANE** is the area between the fingerboard and bridge where the bow is placed:

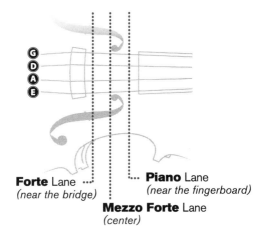

Forte Lane
(near the bridge)

Piano Lane
(near the fingerboard)

Mezzo Forte Lane
(center)

VIOLA

A **BOWING LANE** is the area between the fingerboard and bridge where the bow is placed:

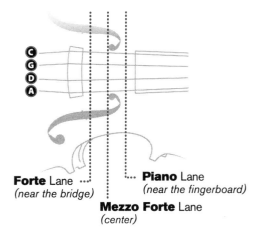

Forte Lane
(near the bridge)

Piano Lane
(near the fingerboard)

Mezzo Forte Lane
(center)

CELLO

A **BOWING LANE** is the area between the fingerboard and bridge where the bow is placed:

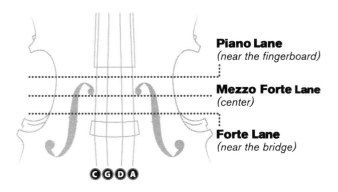

Piano Lane
(near the fingerboard)

Mezzo Forte Lane
(center)

Forte Lane
(near the bridge)

BASS

A **BOWING LANE** is the area between the fingerboard and bridge where the bow is placed:

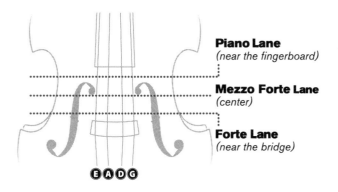

Piano Lane
(near the fingerboard)

Mezzo Forte Lane
(center)

Forte Lane
(near the bridge)

127   **C MAJOR SCALE**—*Play this scale* mezzo forte, *then go back and play it using different dynamic levels.*

SOUND ADVICE

Remind students to watch for dynamic markings. Remind students to watch the DVD for tips on bowing lane placement.

128   **C MAJOR ARPEGGIO**—*Play this* arpeggio forte, *then play it using different dynamic levels.*
What is the interval between the first two notes?

SOUND ADVICE

Remind students to place the bow in the forte lane.

COUNTRY GARDENS—*Play f until p appears in the second measure.*
Circle all the half steps in this piece.

English Folk Song

SOUND ADVICE

Remind students to change bowing lanes when changing dynamics.

130   **SAKURA**—*The word* sakura *refers to spring and the season of the cherry blossom. It is often played on a Japanese stringed instrument called the* koto. *Discuss with your teacher the characteristics of music from different cultures. Listen to the recording of this piece and describe those characteristics.*

SOUND ADVICE

Remind students to look ahead for dynamic changes as they play.

Johann Sebastian Bach (1685–1750) lived during the Baroque era and was one of the world's most prolific composers.

MARCH IN C—*Watch carefully for the* staccato *and* tenuto *markings.*

Johann Sebastian Bach

SOUND ADVICE

Remind students to put separation between the notes marked staccato and to play very smoothly on the notes marked tenuto or legato.

IMPROVISATION is creating music as you play it. *Old Joe Clark* is an American square dance tune. Fiddle players often create their own variations to this song. Make up your own rhythmic variation by playing two eighth notes in place of some of the quarter notes.

132

OLD JOE CLARK—*Violins and violas watch carefully for the high (Hi) 2s and low (Lo) 2s. Cellos and basse watch carefully for the F♯s and C♮s.*

American Fiddle Tune

SOUND ADVICE

Remind students to play with a steady tempo.

Franz Joseph Haydn (1732–1809) wrote his Symphony No. 94 in 1791 during the Classical period. It is sometimes referred to as the "Surprise Symphony" because of the loud note in measure 8.

REHEARSAL MARKS are reference numbers or letters in a box above the staff. They are also called rehearsal numbers or letters.

SURPRISE SYMPHONY—*Watch for the staccato marks, slurs, dynamics, accidentals and bowings. Discuss with your teacher the characteristics of music written during this period of music history. Listen to the recording of this piece and describe those characteristics.*

Franz Joseph Haydn

SOUND ADVICE

Ask students to start the piece in different places by referring to the rehearsal marks.

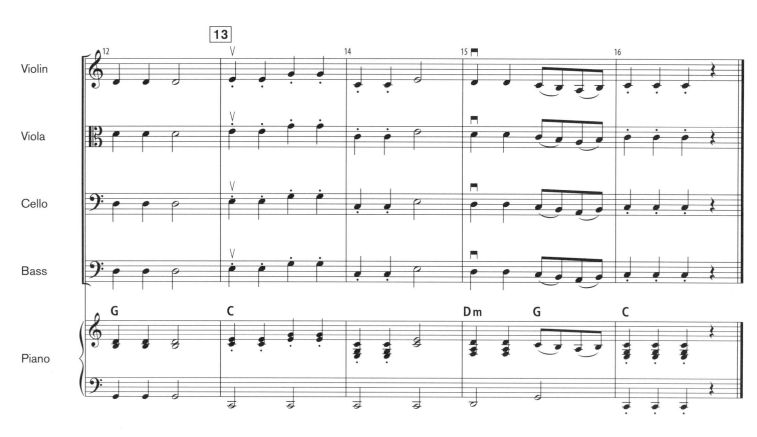

CONDUCTORS lead groups of musicians with specific hand and arm patterns. Each time signature has a different conducting pattern. Practice each of the following patterns with the corresponding pieces below.

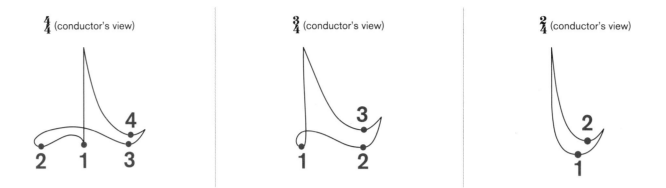

Conducting is simply an extrapolation of one's ability to move to sounds. Students who learn and are encouraged to practice basic conducting skills benefit in a number of profoundly important ways.

▶ Conducting helps students physically represent the metric structure of beats in a measure with their arsis, thesis, stronger, weaker and lifting qualities, rather than simple pulses of equal metric weight.

▶ Through conducting, students learn to mold sounds into fluid phrases by moving to, and feeling the flow, contour, shape, line and inflection of notes within a musical phrase.

▶ The motion of conducting a beat pattern often helps young people improve their sense of steady pulse by physically showing the time between beats.

HUNTER'S CHORUS—*This is conducted with the 4/4 pattern.*

Carl Maria von Weber

SOUND ADVICE

Have all students conduct a 4/4 pattern while listening to the recording of this piece.

135   **MINUET**—*This is conducted with the $\frac{3}{4}$ pattern.*

Johann Sebastian Bach

SOUND ADVICE

Have half of the ensemble conduct while the other half plays, and then reverse.

136   **MUSETTE**—*This is conducted with the $\frac{2}{4}$ pattern.*

Johann Sebastian Bach

SOUND ADVICE

Have individual students stand up and conduct the ensemble.

THEME AND VARIATIONS is a compositional technique in which the composer clearly states a melody (or theme), then changes it by adding contrasting variations.

7 **THEME AND VARIATIONS ON BAA-BAA BLACK SHEEP**—*How does* Variation 1 *differ from the* Theme*? How does* Variation 2 *differ from* Variation 1*?*

SOUND ADVICE

Have students play the variation they composed for each other. Ask them to describe the similarities to and differences from the *Theme*.

Compose your own variation to Baa-Baa Black Sheep. *Notate your variation, then perform it.*

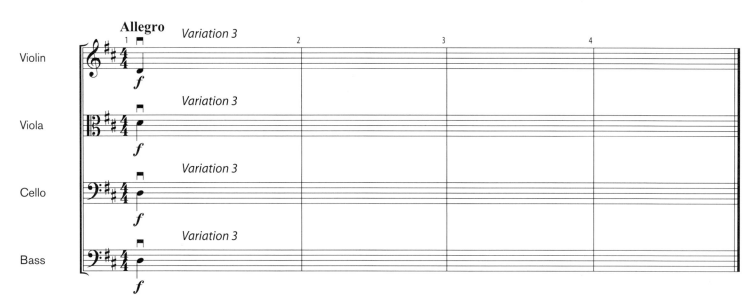

A **WHOLE NOTE** receives 4 beats (counts).

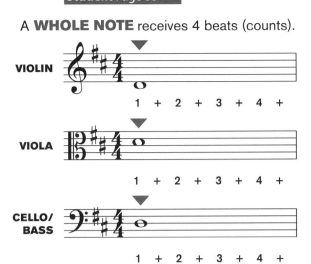

A **WHOLE REST** indicates a full measure of silence.

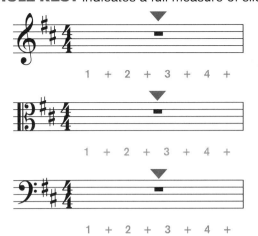

Whole notes can be subdivided into four quarter notes.

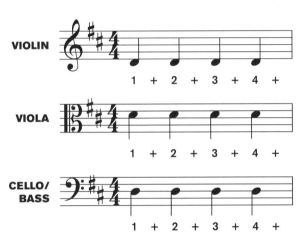

Whole rests in 4/4 time can be subdivided into four quarter rests.

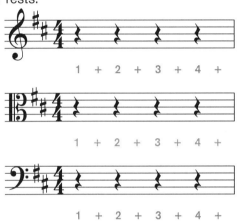

COUNT TO FOUR—*Count carefully.*

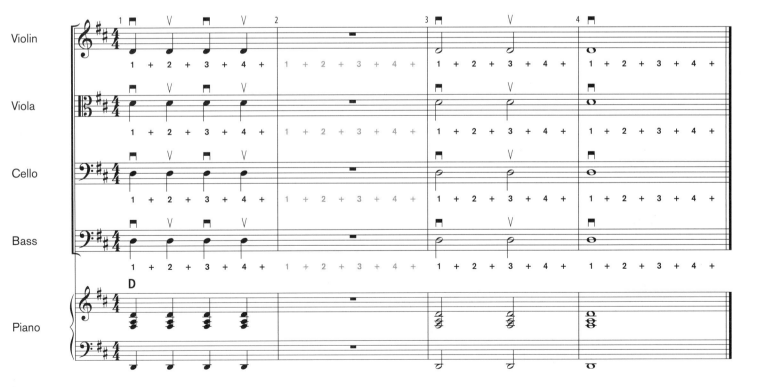

SOUND ADVICE

Remind students to move the bow slowly when playing whole notes, and to count the whole-note rest silently while playing.

Modest Mussorgsky (1839–1881) wrote *Pictures At An Exhibition* as a piano suite, which was later arranged for orchestra by Nikolai Rimsky-Korsakov. The piece depicts a tour through an art gallery. In addition to form and color, music uses many of the same concepts as the visual arts.

139

THE GREAT GATE OF KIEV (FROM PICTURES AT AN EXHIBITION)—*Count silently while you play*

Modest Mussorgsky

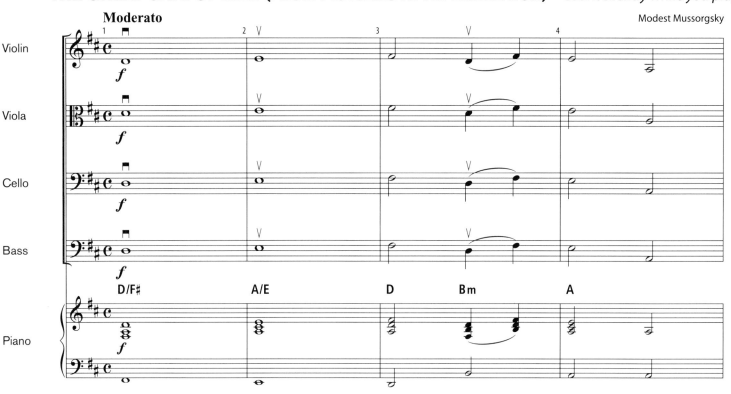

SOUND ADVICE

Remind students to start in the forte lane and use more arm weight.

CHESTER—*Count silently in all the whole-note measures.*

William Billings

SOUND ADVICE

Have students air-bow this piece while listening to the recording.

Reminder: Accidentals last for the entire measure.

A **SHARP** raises the pitch of a note by a half-step.

A **FLAT** lowers the pitch of a note by a half-step. You will learn more about flats in Book 2.

A **NATURAL** cancels a sharp or flat.

A **COURTESY ACCIDENTAL** appears in parentheses as a reminder of the key signature.

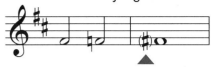

CHROMATICS are a series of notes that move in half steps.

HALF-STEP MARCH—*Circle the accidentals.*

SOUND ADVICE

Ask students to count how many half steps (6) exist in this piece.

142

LAKOTA COURTING SONG—*Native Americans originally played this song on a wooden flute.*

Traditional

SOUND ADVICE

Remind students to look at the tempo marking and all dynamics before playing this piece.

MORNING MOOD FROM PEER GYNT—*How many accidentals are in this piece?*

Edvard Grieg

SOUND ADVICE

Ask students to watch their stand partners play and evaluate if their bow is moving parallel to the bridge.

144 **ACCIDENTAL FRÈRE JACQUES**—*Listen to Accidental Frère Jacques and see if you can hear which notes have been changed from the original melody. Circle those notes.*

French Folk Song

SOUND ADVICE

Have students play this piece as a round by starting two measures apart.

SOUND CHECK Check off each skill you have mastered.

___ Playing dynamics correctly

___ Playing in different meters

___ Playing whole notes

___ Reading accidentals

___ Playing staccatos

___ Conducting in $\frac{4}{4}$, $\frac{3}{4}$, and $\frac{2}{4}$ time.

Level 4: Sound Techniques
E STRING NOTES

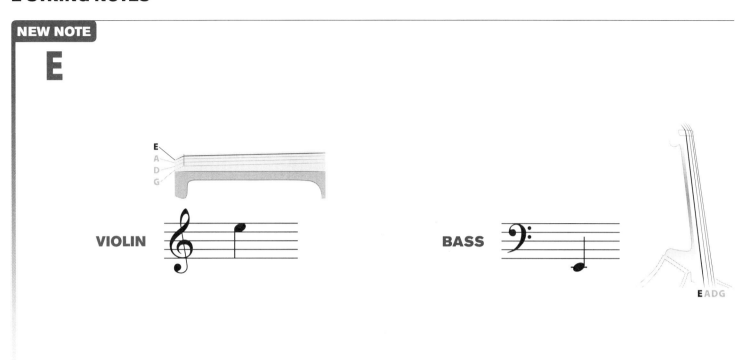

VIOLIN

BASS

-5 **NEW NOTE OPEN E STRING FOR VIOLINS AND BASSES**—*Violas and cellos review.*

Violin

Viola

Cello

Bass

Piano

SOUND ADVICE

Remind students to watch the DVD to review tips on finger placement.

NEW NOTE

B

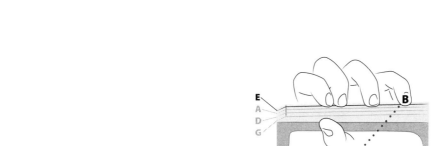

VIOLIN

146   **NEW NOTE B FOR VIOLINS**—*Violas, cellos and basses review.*

SOUND ADVICE

Remind violins to pull the left elbow under the neck when playing 4th-finger B.

NEW NOTE

A

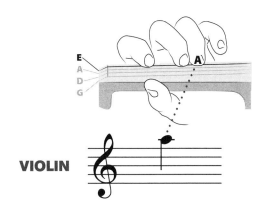

VIOLIN

7   **NEW NOTE A FOR VIOLINS**—*Violas, cellos and basses review.*

SOUND ADVICE

Ask violins to compare the 3rd finger A with the open A string to check intonation.

NEW NOTE

G

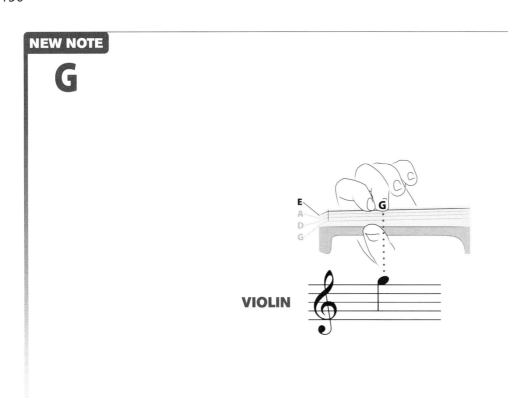

VIOLIN

148   **NEW NOTE G FOR VIOLINS**—*Violas, cellos and basses review.*

SOUND ADVICE

Remind violins that G on the E string is played with a Lo 2 finger pattern.

F♯

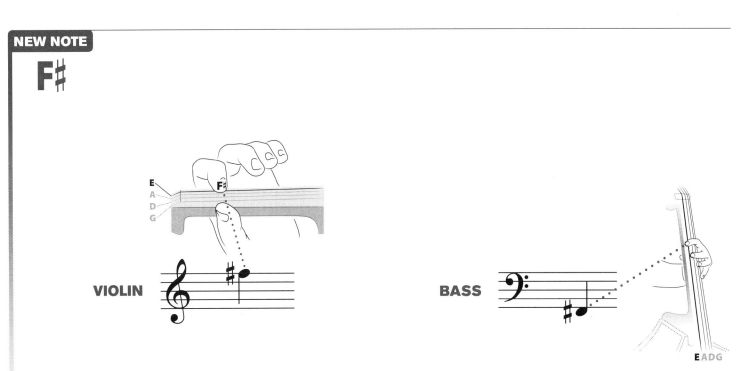

VIOLIN

BASS

9

NEW NOTE F♯ FOR VIOLINS AND BASSES—*Violas and cellos review.*

SOUND ADVICE

Remind basses to keep the left elbow up when playing 1st finger F♯.

NEW NOTE

E

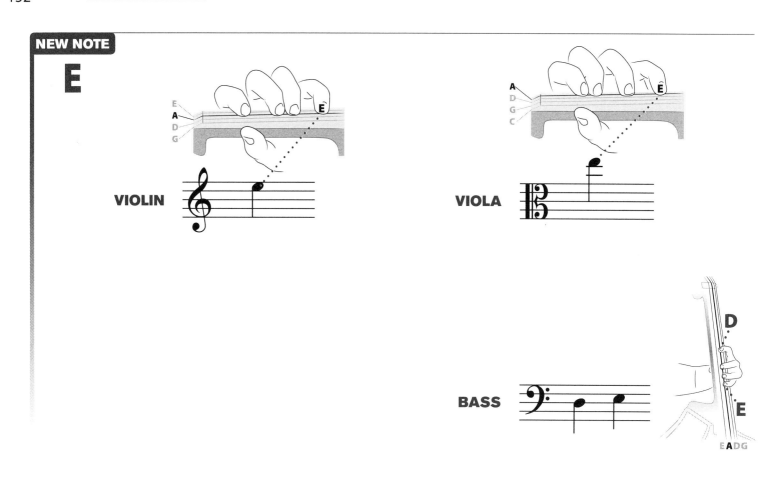

150   **NEW NOTE E FOR VIOLINS, VIOLAS AND BASSES**—*Cellos review.*

SOUND ADVICE

Remind violas to pull the left elbow under the neck when playing 4th finger E. Remind basses to use more arm weight in the bow when playing E.

1

COMING DOWN THE E STRING—*Walking down the E string for violins and basses.*
Violas and cellos review.

SOUND ADVICE

Remind basses to hold the instrument so they can easily bow the E string.

2

GOING UP THE E STRING—*Walking up the E string for violins and basses. Violas and cellos review.*

SOUND ADVICE

Remind the violins to use less arm weight when playing on the E string.

153 **G MAJOR SCALE**—*Play the second octave of a G Major scale for violins. Violas, cellos and basses review.*

SOUND ADVICE

Remind the violins to listen to the other sections in the ensemble while playing the upper octave G scale. Remind basses to watch the DVD to review tips on finger placement.

MAJOR and **MINOR KEYS**—Most of the music we hear is either in a major or minor key. The mood of a major key is often cheerful or heroic, while a minor key may be somber or solemn. The sound of the key is created by the arrangement of half steps and whole steps.

FORTE-PIANO (*f-p*) indicates to play *forte* the first time, and then *piano* on the repeat.

4

AURA LEE—*Practice your new dynamics and notes. Does this piece sound like it is in a major or a minor key?*

American Folk Song

SOUND ADVICE

Have students find the correct height and placement of the music stand to ensure good posture and playing position, as well as the ability to watch you.

155 **THE ERIE CANAL**—*Violins and basses play on the E string while violas and cellos review.*
Does this piece sound like it is in a major or minor key?
Do not repeat the first section on the D.C..

American Folk Song

SOUND ADVICE

Remind students that *f–p* means to play forte the first time and piano the second time.

C STRING NOTES

NEW NOTE

C

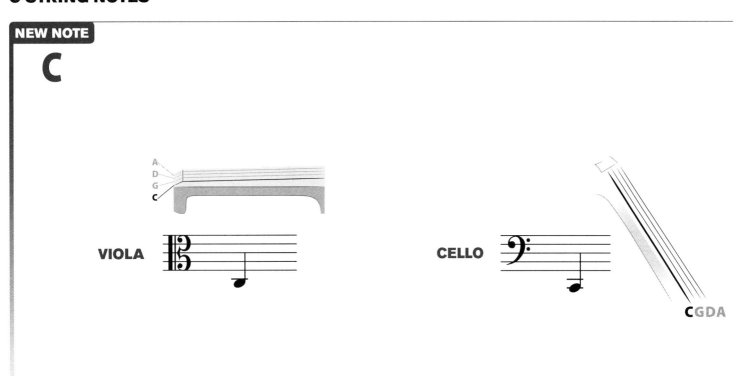

VIOLA

CELLO

CGDA

6   **NEW NOTE OPEN C STRING FOR VIOLAS AND CELLOS**—*Violins and basses review.*

SOUND ADVICE

Remind students to watch the DVD to review tips on finger placement.

NEW NOTE

F

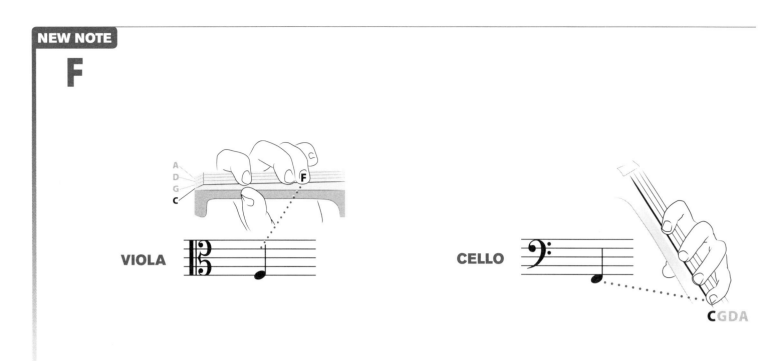

VIOLA   CELLO

157   **NEW NOTE F FOR VIOLAS AND CELLOS**—*Violins and basses review.*

SOUND ADVICE

Remind violas and cellos to move the left arm to the correct bow level to play on the C string.

NEW NOTE

E

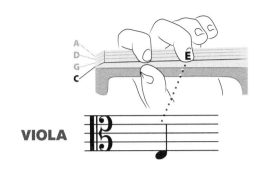

VIOLA

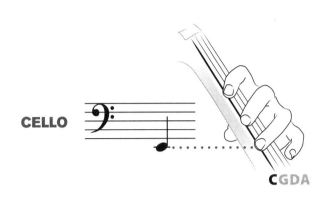

CELLO

NEW NOTE E FOR VIOLAS AND CELLOS—*Violins and basses review.*

SOUND ADVICE

Remind the violas and cellos to use more left-arm weight when playing on the C string.

NEW NOTE

D

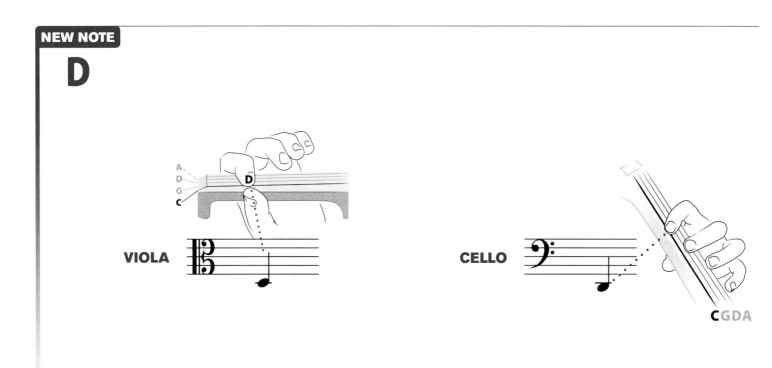

VIOLA   CELLO

159   **NEW NOTE D FOR VIOLAS AND CELLOS**—*Violins and basses review.*

SOUND ADVICE

Have violas and cellos check the 1st finger D with the open D string for intonation.

NEW NOTE
G

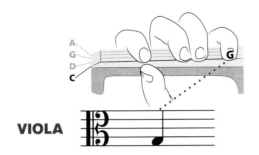

VIOLA

0

NEW NOTE G FOR VIOLAS—*Violins, cellos and basses review.*

SOUND ADVICE

Remind violas to pull the left elbow under the neck when playing G on the C string.

161 **COMING DOWN THE C STRING**—*Walking down the C string for violas and cellos. Violins and basses review.*

SOUND ADVICE

Remind cellos to keep the left arm up when playing on the C string.

162 **GOING UP THE C STRING**—*Walking up the C string for violas and cellos. Violins and basses review.*

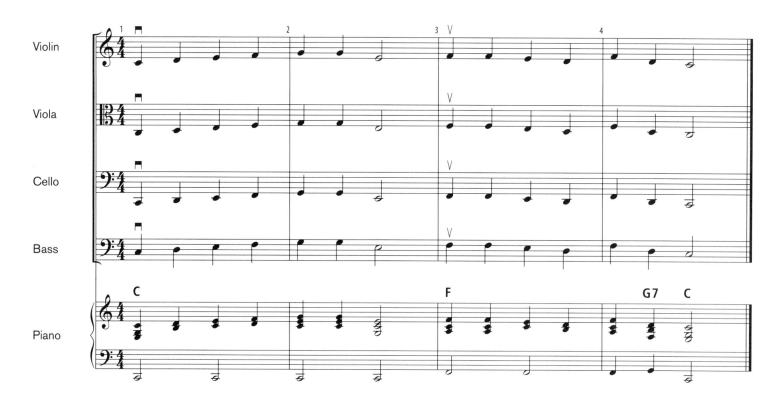

SOUND ADVICE

Remind violas to hold the instrument parallel to the floor when playing on the C string.

3   **C STRING JUMPS**—*Skipping on the C string for violas and cellos. Violins and basses review.*

SOUND ADVICE

Remind students to play with a beautiful tone.

4   **C MAJOR SCALE ON THE C STRING**—*Violas and cellos begin on the C string. Violins begin on the G string. Basses begin on the A string.*

SOUND ADVICE

Remind students to listen carefully for intonation when playing scales.

165   **C MAJOR SCALE AGAIN**—*The second octave of a C Major scale for violas and cellos. Violins and basses review.*

SOUND ADVICE

Remind students to play this scale starting in the lower half of the bow.

TEXIAN BOYS—*Practice playing on the C string for violas and cellos.*

Texas Folk Song

SOUND ADVICE

Remind students not to change tempo when moving from less active to more active rhythms within a passage.

167

SWEETLY SINGS THE DONKEY—*Practice playing on the C string for violas and cellos.*
Circle each rest. This can be played as a round.

American Folk Song

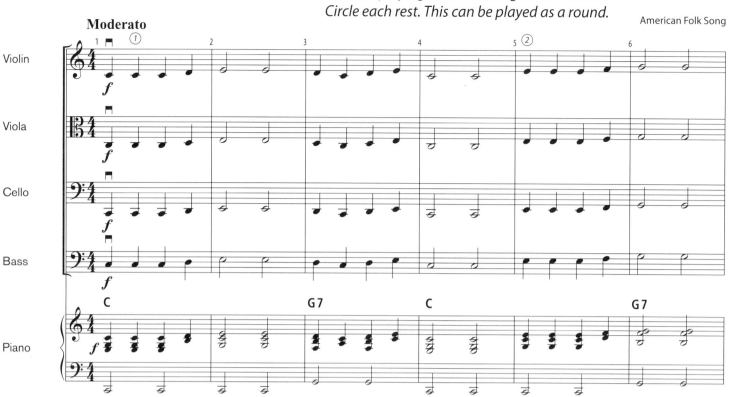

SOUND ADVICE

When starting this piece, remind the violas and cellos to let their bow sink firmly into the C string.

SOUND CHECK Check off each skill you have mastered.

___ E string notes (violins and basses)   ___ C string notes (violas and cellos)
___ Playing *f-p*   ___ Playing in a minor key
___ Playing in a major key   ___ Playing with a correct bow hold

Level 5: Sound Development

An **EIGHTH REST** receives half a beat (count) of silence. A quarter rest can be subdivided into two eighth rests.

Remember, an eighth note receives half a beat (count). An eighth note with an eighth rest is written like this:

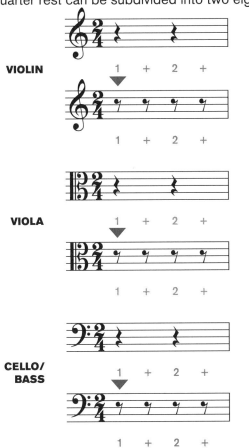

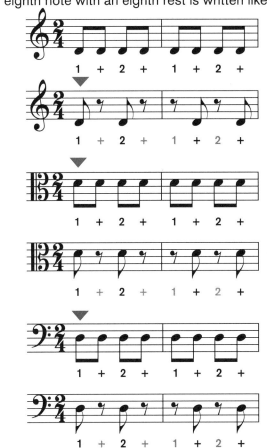

EIGHTH RESTS—*Clap while counting aloud. Next, sing and then play the piece.*

SOUND ADVICE

Have students clap the piece while counting aloud.

Student Page 41

169   **SINGLE EIGHTH NOTES AND RESTS**—*Clap while counting aloud. Next, sing and then play the pie*

SOUND ADVICE

Remind students to stop the bow before each eighth rest.

170   **ALOUETTE**—*Count silently while playing.*

French Folk Song

SOUND ADVICE

Remind students to count during rests.

1   **RESTING AGAIN**—*Play eighth notes and rests in ¼ time.*

SOUND ADVICE

Remind students to stop the bow when playing a single eighth note followed by a single eighth rest.

MAY SONG—*Which measures have an eighth note rest in them?*

Folk Song

SOUND ADVICE

Remind students to move the bow quickly when playing the single eighth notes after the single eighth rest.

A **DOTTED QUARTER NOTE** receives 1½ beats. Dotted quarter notes can be subdivded into three eighth notes.

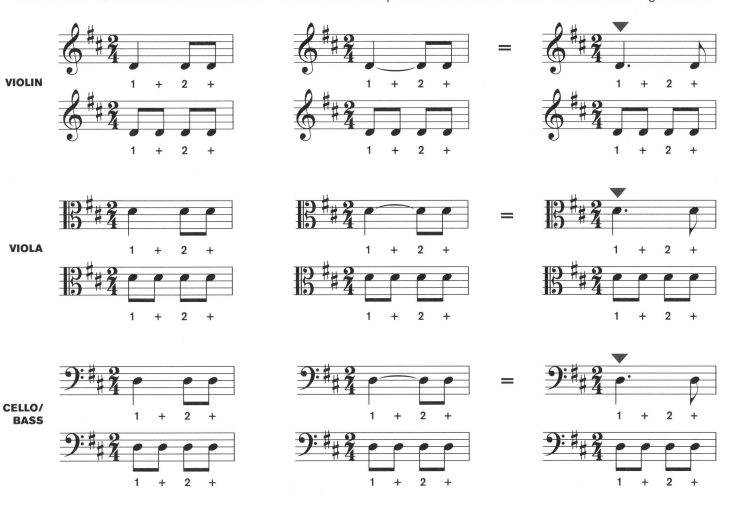

PLAYING DOTTED QUARTER NOTES—*Clap while counting aloud. Next, sing and then play the piece.*

SOUND ADVICE

Remind students to play the dotted quarter note for its full value.

174

SLURRING DOTTED QUARTER NOTES—*Clap while counting aloud.*
Next, sing and then play the piece.

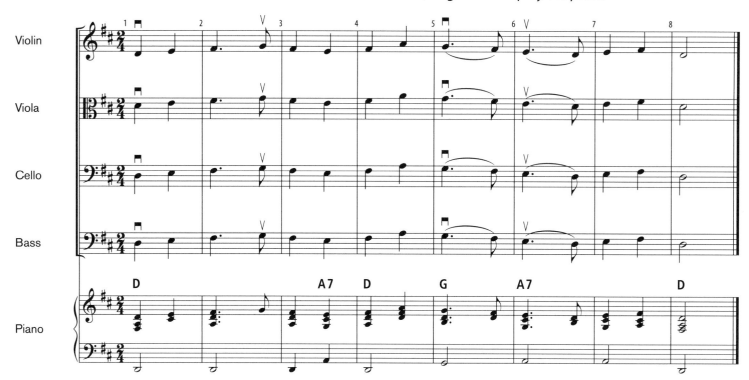

SOUND ADVICE

Remind students to count the dotted quarter note and eighth note carefully when slurring.

5

SKYE BOAT SONG—*Playing dotted quarters notes in ¾ time.*

Scottish Folk Song

SOUND ADVICE

Point out to students that the bow is moving in a half-note rhythm when playing a slurred dotted quarter note followed by an eighth note.

176   **FINNEGAN'S WAKE**—*How many dotted quarter notes are there in this piece?*

Irish Reel

SOUND ADVICE

Remind students to move the bow more slowly on the dotted quarter note and more quickly on the eighth note that follows it.

The theme, *Going Home*, is from Antonín Dvořák's (1841–1904) symphony, *From the New World*, written while he was visiting America between 1892 and 1895.

177   **GOING HOME**—*Count silently while playing.*

Antonín Dvořák

SOUND ADVICE

Remind students to press the left-hand fingers firmly down when playing at a piano dynamic level.

LEARNING TO PLAY DOUBLE STOPS—*A double stop is when two strings are played at the same time.*

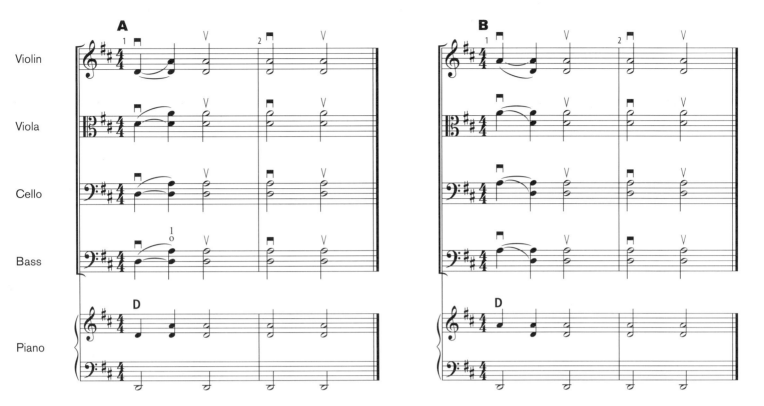

SOUND ADVICE

Remind students to keep the bow weight even on both strings of the double stop.

DOUBLE THE FUN—*In order to play double stops with the fingers down, create a tunnel over the open A string with your fingers. While playing a double stop, check the tunnel by plucking the open A string to make sure it rings for violins, violas and cellos. Basses review.*

SOUND ADVICE

Ask students to check the "tunnel" of their stand partner.

180   **BOIL THEM CABBAGE DOWN WITH DOUBLE STOPS**—*Play this tune by fingering the lower note on the D string and playing the open A string at the same time for violins, violas and cellos. This is often done in fiddle music. Basses play the melody only.*

American Fiddle Tune

SOUND ADVICE

Remind students that the left-hand fingers will make a tunnel over the open A string.

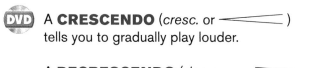 A **CRESCENDO** (*cresc.* or ————) tells you to gradually play louder.

A **DECRESCENDO** (*decresc.* or —————) tells you to gradually play softer.

A **RITARDANDO** (*rit.*) or **RALLENTANDO** (*rall.*) tells you to gradually slow down.

A **FERMATA** (𝄐) tells you to hold the note longer than its normal value.

THE YELLOW ROSE OF TEXAS—*Practice playing the crescendos, decrescendos, ritardando and fermata. This piece is often referred to as the unofficial state song of Texas.*

Texas Folk Song by J. K.

SOUND ADVICE

Have students point to each blue wedge and explain what they mean to their stand partner.

SOUND CHECK Check off each skill you have mastered.

___ Playing single eighth notes and rests
___ Playing double stops
___ Playing a ritardando

___ Playing and reading dotted quarter notes
___ Playing a crescendo and decrescendo
___ Playing a fermata

Level 6: Sound Performance

Much like a duet, an **ORCHESTRA ARRANGEMENT** includes separate parts for different members of the ensemble to play. Take turns performing *Sword Dance* while others in your class evaluate the performance using criteria developed with your teacher. Some things to evaluate may include rhythm, intonation, tone, dynamics, phrasing and expression.

Orchestra Arrangement

SWORD DANCE—*When are you playing the melody, and when are you playing the harmony?*

Renaissance Dance Tune

SOUND ADVICE

Remind students to listen to each other and make sure the melody is heard at all times no matter which part of the orchestra plays it.

Develop a list of good concert etiquette rules. Some things to include might be to listen quietly and to show your appreciation by applauding at the end of the piece. Take turns performing *Sourwood Mountain* while others in your class practice good concert etiquette. Notice in this arrangement you have a choice of two parts. Your teacher will tell you which part to play.

183   **SOURWOOD MOUNTAIN**

American Fiddle Tune

SOUND ADVICE

Assign students to play either the melody or accompaniment line.

184 The **BLUES** is an American art form derived from spirituals and work songs. It is the root of rock and roll, bluegrass and jazz. Notice in this arrangement you have a choice of two parts. Your teacher will tell you which part to play in *Perpetual Rock Motion.*

ORCHESTRA ARRANGEMENT

PERPETUAL ROCK MOTION

SOUND ADVICE

Have all students play the melody, then the accompaniment line. Now go back and assign part of the ensemble to play the melody and the others to play the accompaniment.

VIOLIN
PENTATONIC SCALE—*What is different about this scale?*

Using the notes in the pentatonic scale (a scale with only five notes), improvise your own solo or melody for *Perpetual Rock Motion*. Play it while your friends play the harmony part.

VIOLA
PENTATONIC SCALE—*What is different about this scale?*

Using the notes in the pentatonic scale (a scale with only five notes), improvise your own solo or melody for *Perpetual Rock Motion*. Play it while your friends play the harmony part.

CELLO/BASS
PENTATONIC SCALE—*What is different about this scale?*

Using the notes in the pentatonic scale (a scale with only five notes), improvise your own solo or melody for *Perpetual Rock Motion*. Play it while your friends play the harmony part.

SOUND ADVICE
The student books contain three blank staff lines so they can use the notes in the pentatonic scale to compose their own melody to *Perpetual Rock Motion*. They should create and notate the rhythm first, then the melody.

A **SOLO** is a piece that is performed alone or with accompaniment. Before playing this piece, watch and listen to it being performed on the DVD.

Many factors go into creating a great performance. Develop a list of things you think a performer should do to prepare for a performance. You might include such things as being on time, being prepared and practicing.

185 GAVOTTE—*Solo*

Arcangelo Corelli

SOUND ADVICE

Remind students to watch the DVD performance of the final solo piece. Have an in-class recital in which all students get a chance to perform this solo.

PRINCE OF DENMARK'S MARCH—*Solo* 🔘 **DVD**

Jeremiah Clarke

rit. last time only

Fine

rit. last time only

D.C. al Fine

SOUND ADVICE

Remind students to watch the DVD performance of the final solo piece. Have an in-class recital in which all students get a chance to perform this solo.

185 **CHORUS FROM "JUDAS MACCABEUS"**—*Solo* **DVD**

George Frideric Handel (1685–1759)

SOUND ADVICE

Remind students to watch the DVD performance of the final solo piece. Have an in-class recital in which all students get a chance to perform this solo.

RIGAUDON—*Solo*

Henry Purcell

SOUND ADVICE

Remind students to watch the DVD performance of the final solo piece. Have an in-class recital in which all students get a chance to perform this solo.

SOUND CHECK Check off each skill you have mastered.

___ Playing in parts   ___ Improvising

___ Playing a solo   ___ Being a good performer

___ Composing a melody   ___ Demonstrating good concert etiquette

190

Glossary

1st and 2nd endings – play the 1st ending the first time through; repeat the music, but skip over the 1st ending on the repeat and play the 2nd ending instead

accent (>) – play the note with a strong attack

accidentals (♯, ♭, ♮) – *see page 4*

allegro – a fast tempo

alto clef – indicates the third line of the staff is middle C

andante – a slow tempo

arco – to play with the bow

arpeggio – the notes of a chord played one after another

bass clef – indicates the fourth line of the staff is F

blues – an American art form derived from spirituals and work songs; it is the root of rock and roll, bluegrass and jazz

bow lift (ʼ) – to raise the bow off the string and reset it on the string

bow speed – how fast or slowly the bow moves across the string

bowing lanes – the contact points between the bridge and the fingerboard where the bow is placed; the center lane is halfway between the bridge and the fingerboard

chord – three or more notes played at the same time

chromatics – a series of notes that move in half steps

concerto – a composition for orchestra and soloist

conductor – leads groups of musicians with specific hand and arm patterns

courtesy accidentals – appear in parentheses as a reminder of the key signature

crescendo – gradually play louder

D.C. al Fine – repeat from the beginning and play to the *Fine*

decrescendo – gradually play softer

dot – increases the length of a note by half its value

double bar line – indicates the end of a section

down bow (⊓) – to pull the bow down by moving your hand to the right (away from your body)

duet – a composition for two performers

dynamics – changes in volume

fermata (⌢) – hold the note longer than its normal value

Fine – the end of a piece of music

forte (*f*) – play loudly

forte-piano (*f-p*) – indicates to play forte the first time, and then piano on the repeat

half step – the smallest distance between two notes

hooked bowing – a curved line above or below two notes with staccato marks; it tells you to play the notes with stops in the same bow direction

improvisation – creating music as you play

interval – the distance between two notes

key signature – appears at the beginning of the staff, and indicates which notes will be played sharp or flat

ledger line – short, horizontal line used to extend a staff either higher or lower

left-facing repeat – indicates to go back to the beginning or to the closest right-facing repeat

left-hand pizzicato (+) – pluck the string with the 4th finger of the left hand

mezzo forte (*mf*) – medium loud

moderato – a moderate tempo

octave – the interval of an 8th

pentatonic scale – a scale having five notes

piano (*p*) – play softly

pickup – a note (or notes) that occurs before the first complete measure of a piece

rallentando – becoming gradually slower

rehearsal mark – reference number or letter in a box above the staff

right-facing repeat – indicates the first measure of the section to be repeated

ritardando – becoming gradually slower

round – music in which players start the piece at different times, creating interesting harmonies and accompaniments

scale – usually a series of eight notes that go up or down the musical alphabet in a specific order of whole steps and half steps; the lowest and highest notes of the scale are always the same letter name

slur – a curved line placed above or below two or more different notes; it tells you to play the notes smoothly in the same bow direction

solo – a piece that is performed alone or with accompaniment

staccato (·) – play short and detached; separate the notes by stopping the bow

tempo marking – indicates the speed of the music

tenuto (legato) (–) – hold the note for its full value and play smoothly

theme – a central musical idea or melody

theme and variations – a compositional technique in which the composer clearly states a melody (theme), then changes it by adding contrasting variations

tie – a curved line that connects two or more notes of the same pitch; the tied notes are played as one longer note with the combined value of both notes

time signature or meter – indicates the number of beats (counts) in each measure and the type of note that receives one beat

treble clef – indicates second line of the staff is G

up bow (∨) – to push the bow up by moving your hand to the left (toward your body)

Violin Fingering Chart

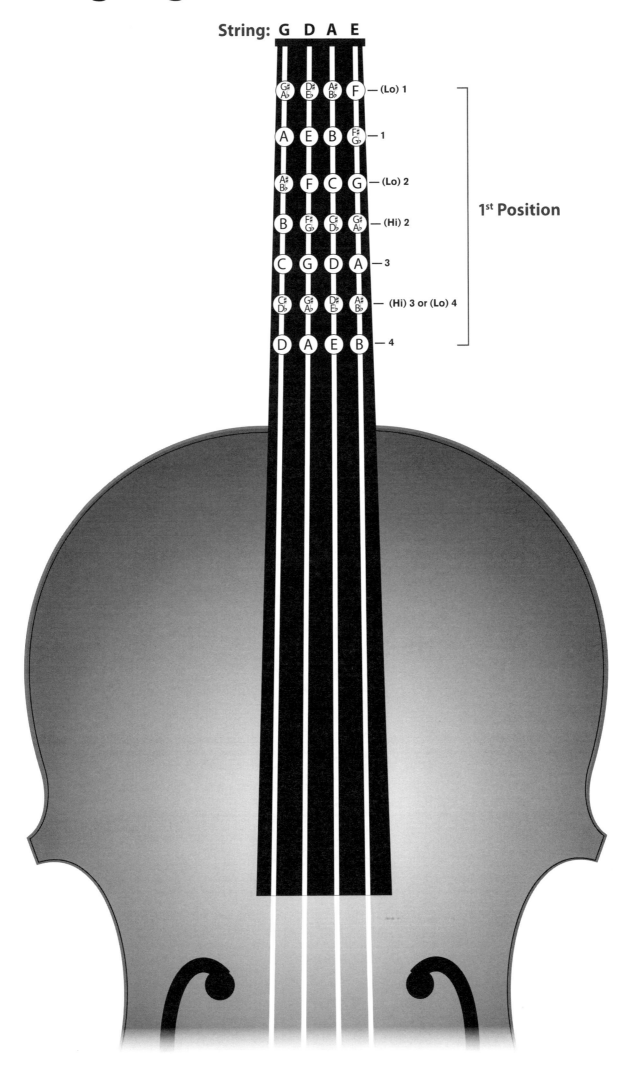

Viola Fingering Chart

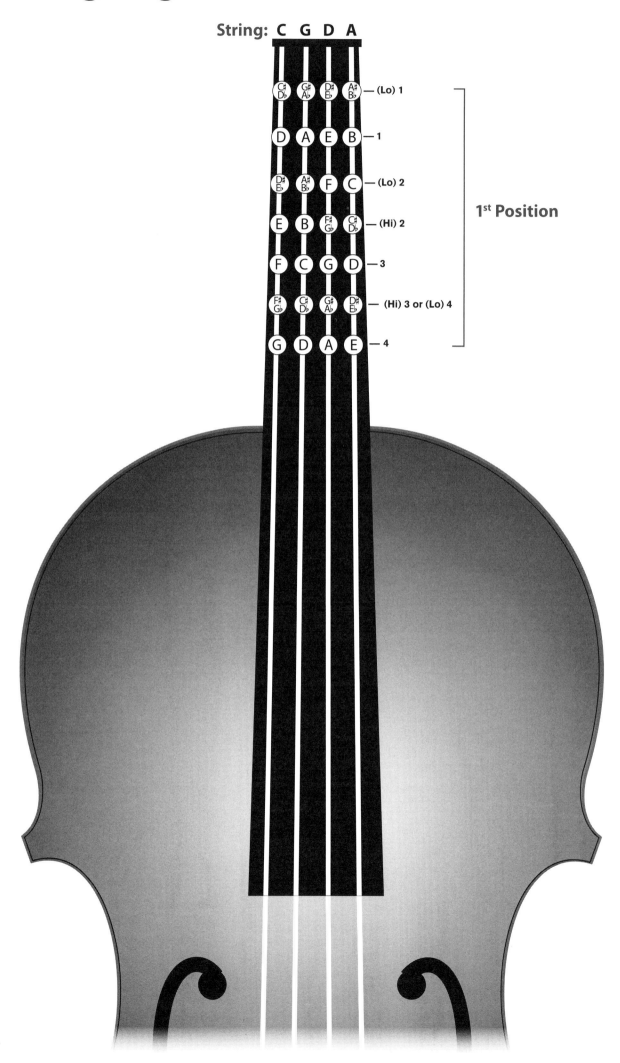

Cello Fingering Chart

Bass Fingering Chart

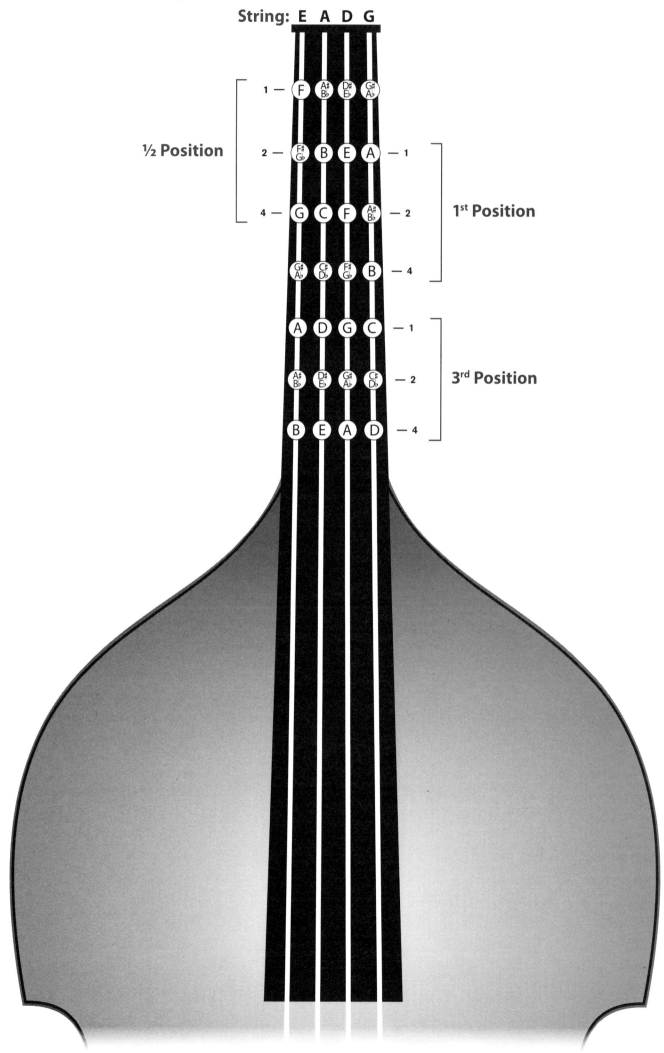

Practice Record

Name _____

Class (Day/Time) _____

To become a good musician, you must practice every day. Find a convenient place where you can keep your instrument, book, music, and any other practice equipment. Try to practice at the same time every day. To help you schedule your time, use this daily practice record.

Week	Date	Assignment	Mon	Tue	Wed	Thur	Fri	Sat	Sun	Total	Parent/Teacher Signature
1											
2											
3											
4											
5											
6											
7											
8											
9											
10											
11											
12											
13											
14											
15											
16											
17											
18											
19											
20											
21											
22											
23											
24											
25											
26											
27											
28											
29											
30											
31											
32											
33											
34											
35											
36											
37											
38											

*The authors would like to thank the following for their involvement
in producing the Sound Innovations Standard Edition books:*

Jon Senge, Engraving

Matt Koprowski, Art, Design and Technical Support

Dana D'Elia, Art and Design

Eric Fortin, New Media Support and SI Player Programming

John O'Reilly, Consulting Editor

Pam Phillips, Project Manager

Derek Richard, Director of Production

SOUND

™

INNOVATIONS

Certificate of Completion

This certifies that

has successfully completed

Sound Innovations for String Orchestra, Book 1

_____

Teacher/Parent

_____

Date